BeTween
Everything

beTween everything

Teacher Helps for Transitioning Preteens

Ed Trimmer and Patty Meyers

BeTween Everything
Teacher Helps for Transitioning Preteens

Copyright © 2004 Abingdon Press

ISBN 0-687-05828-7

04 05 06 07 08 09 10 11 12 13 — 10 9 8 7 6 5 4 3 2 1

MANUFACTURED IN THE UNITED STATES OF AMERICA

To
Peggy and Bob

Our Spouses and Partners in Ministry

With Appreciation

CONTENTS

INTRODUCTION

So What's a *Tween?*

If you are sports fans like us, the term *tween* conjures up the basketball player who is too small to play forward and to slow to be a guard—a classic *tweener*. Our computer people refer to a *tweener* as not a computer but between a laptop and a hand held PDA. USA Today called those born between 1960 and 1965 *tweeners*, another word to describe the group somewhere between the Baby Boomers and Generation X ("Stuck between Generations," Andrea Stone; March 22-24, 1996). We are interested in *tweens*, not *tweeners*. There is some general confusion about these terms, and some have used the terms for each other, so one must be careful about the use of the term.

What Does *Tween* Mean To You?

We are going to refer to and focus on *tweens*, those in grades five through seven, particularly those in fifth and sixth grade. Classic *tweens* are people who seem not to be children any more (just ask them!) and too young to be in youth group. Increasingly we hear the term *tween* being used to refer to those from ages nine through twelve. They're nine to twelve going on seventeen or eighteen. Not kids, not teens, they're tweens.

> ## Not kids, not teens, they're tweens.

The Institute for International Research says about tweens: "Viewing themselves as sophisticated and mature, they have an attitude that's all their own. Tweens have become one of the nation's most significant consumer groups. Huge amounts of music, television, movies, games, electronics, fashion and food are being marketed in their direction - and they're buying!"[1]

So What Are We Going To Do?

The church has an older definition of youth as those from age "12-18 ...and generally in the seventh grade through the twelfth grade" (*Book of Discipline of the United Methodist Church*; United Methodist Publishing House, 2000; p. 255.2). Most mainline denominations have similar definitions. However, some organizations have gone to very specialized definition of youth and children where they focus on smaller and smaller groups, such as kids, ages 4-8; tweens, ages 9-12; early adolescents, ages 12-14; middle adolescents, ages 15-17; and late adolescents, ages 17-19.

> The middle school concept is coming under more and more scrutiny.

Some tweens will be in a middle school, while others are still in elementary school. Even as we write, the middle school concept is coming under more and more scrutiny with the publication of new books like *The War Against Excellence: The Rising Tide of Mediocrity in America's Middle Schools* by Cheri Pierson Yecke (Greenwood Publishing Group, Inc., 2003). How this new scrutiny will affect tweens and the schools they inhabit is not yet clear, but the scrutiny and the changes in middle schools will be significant and will affect tweens.

The Carnegie Foundation has used the age range of 10-19 years to describe youth. However, most youth ministries in local churches have been organized around the school and have typically not included ten and eleven or even twelve year olds, especially if they are still in an elementary school.

This book addresses these tweens, who they are, how we can help them make a better transition into adolescence, and how we can help them engage their faith in meaningful ways. To do this, we have divided our study into seven units of study and reflection.

First, we will look at physical development of tweens, and especially how this affects teaching. Then we will look at cognitive development and how it affects teaching, lifting up helpful information from recent brain research. Then we will look at socio-emotional development as it affects teaching. These three units focus on what is happening internally in a tween. Next, we will look at the environment that surrounds the tween and focus on cultural issues such as parenting, media, peer relationships (including sibling relationships), and of course, school. Then we will put all of this together in relationship to how faith develops and is nurtured, how tweens learn, and how teachers and leaders can work with them for optimal outcomes. Finally, we share some brief and practical advice on teaching tweens, building on the previous units' practical advice and ideas.

Quentin J. Schultze writes in *Winning Your Kids Back From the Media*, "Every time I go to the local shopping mall I feel greater confusion: older women seem to be acting and dressing like younger and younger ones, while ever younger girls seem to be dressing and acting like older ones.... I am not always sure when childhood ends and adulthood begins" (InterVarsity Press, 1994; p. 144). Tweens are those persons who may act like adults one day, especially in their dress and language, but the next day enjoy being pushed on swings. Tweens may no longer be children, but they are not quite teenagers.

Sometime in their tween years they will begin to experience life as an emotional roller coaster (some more than others). Each tween is an individual with a unique personality and a developmental timeline of his or her own. So when these developmental issues emerge is different for each tween. How they respond to these developmental issues is different, but there are some common issues that we want to help you understand that will help you be a better teacher and a better adult mentor to tweens in their lives and their Christian journeys. Ultimately tweens are kids, part of God's creation, vacillating between delightful cooperation and frustrating stubbornness. They are to be loved, nurtured and held up as precious in God's sight.

> Each tween is an individual with a unique personality and a developmental timeline of his or her own.

So What Should We Remember?

We ought to always remember that no matter what, God created people of all ages and calls them by name. All of God's children need:

▶ Love
▶ A sense of self-worth
▶ A sense of accomplishment
▶ A safe place to risk being who they really are
▶ Opportunities to practice being what they are and will become
▶ A place to be surrounded by people who model God's love for them
▶ To experience that love for themselves first hand

Those who believe and call themselves by the name of God's son, Jesus Christ—Christians—are members of his body, the Church. As "members one of the other," we act on behalf of Christ to help meet those needs. People of faith make a difference! Be sure that you include all of these with tweens because one of their greatest needs is for success.

> One of their greatest needs is for success.

Tween time is a wonderful life stage. It's a time traditionally known for life's turning points, commonly called rites of passage, that are full of transitions. Many religions and traditions recognize the need for girls and boys to take on new and more grown up roles at this stage of life. Bar and bat mitzvahs for Jewish young people and confirmation for Christians are but two examples. Many Christians and churches have pushed these rites of passage earlier and earlier in life, and now they often occur in this new tween time.

Physical changes are only the tip of the iceberg of all the changes that tweens experience. Growth comes in spurts. They are chagrined when their friends seem to grow two inches over the summer and they don't. They are self-conscious when they grow two inches over the summer and their friends don't. Hormones change and affect their emotions. Cognitive abilities change, as do their social interactions.

Girls need special attention. This is the stage when girls, who previously developed faster than boys, often start to have lower self-esteem than boys. They essentially hold themselves back. Researchers say that because they see that their culture values boys more than girls, and because of changing gender roles, they will often not participate at the same level nor perform at the same academic level that they formerly did. Girls may have their first periods as young as age ten, before they are ready to cope with the effects on their bodies, their emotions, and their relationships with their friends of both genders.

Boys need special attention as well. Boys end up dropping out of school and getting in trouble with the law at a much greater rate than girls. Many boys find schoolwork to be unproductive and often begin to turn to drugs for a variety of reasons including self-medication. Many of the vast changes that boys experience during this time period can affect their self-esteem and vision of life.

Many of the characteristics previously associated with teenagers happen now in the tween years. The fast-paced world in which we all live affects these people, too. They reflect the pace of the adults in their world. Parents juggle PDA's and date books, their own schedules with those of their children, their jobs and their homes, and often their own parents. Days start early and end late. Girls and boys juggle along with their parents. Latchkey kids are the norm rather than the exception in many communities.

The common denominator for tweens is change. This is a time of transition in every aspect of their lives. White water rafting might be a good metaphor for what tweens and those who care for them go through. Helping them successfully navigate through these rough waters is an exciting challenge.

Tween time is not only a transitional time, it is also a vulnerable one. Girls and boys in this stage deserve our best efforts. We hope that these young people will grow in their faith, their knowledge of God, themselves, and others, as

> **Tween time is not only a transitional time, it is also a vulnerable one.**

well as the Bible. We hope that they will experience a supportive, caring community as they go through the changes that are inherent in this stage of life. We hope that they will grow in their identity as Christians and members of God's family. To be a parent, teacher or leader of tweens may seem like a mixed blessing, as it is often very hard work. We encourage you to accept the challenge. The rewards are enormously satisfying, and besides, the tween time passes so quickly, it will be over before you know it.

Blessings to you, your tween, and the tweens you teach!

Ed and Patty

So let's get started!

[1]"For those thinking there is no reason to market to shoppers younger than 13, there are 10 billion reasons to change your mind. That's how many dollars children ages 8 to 12—called 'tweens' in marketing parlance—spend every year. They influence another $250 billion in purchases, making them one of the new target markets for companies throughout the country. That has led to a blizzard of new products. The targets: kids and the mothers who take them shopping. 'We talk about a four-eyed, four-legged consumer, mom plus kid,' said Dave Siegel, president of Cincinnati marketing firm WonderGroup, which specializes in marketing to kids."
Reported in *The Cincinnati Enquirer,* March 14, 2003.

Chapter One

PHYSICAL DEVELOPMENT

Introduction

Tweens are on the verge of adolescence, too old and sophisticated to be children anymore, yet in many ways too young to be truly adolescents. However, American culture has fostered a new developmental age that some have called preadolescence—tweens. Many recent chronicles of American cultural life have noted that the period of adolescence seems to begin earlier and last longer for many American young people. In fact, some have argued that the entire concept of adolescent is an invention of the past century that has been promoted by American cultural life (*Dancing in the Dark*, Schultze, Anker and others; Eerdmans Publishing, 1991).

Some of these tweens (nine to twelve year olds) relish the cultural freedoms that have appeared of late, such as dating, attending parties, and shopping by themselves, especially for school clothes and fashions, but others have felt pushed into this new freedom and are not yet ready for, nor desire, the marketing attention, the dating scene, and the trappings of adolescence.

Teachers and leaders must realize that the developmental changes at this age, including physical, emotional, mental, social, and spiritual changes, vary with each individual tween. Thus each tween needs to be understood as a distinct individual with tremendous variance in development. It is difficult to generalize about developmental changes, for while they will occur (in most individuals), tweens each have their own timetable. We must love tweens as they vacillate between delightful cooperation and frustrating stubbornness. It may help to recall that Jesus was a tween when he began his ministry. It was at this time

> Each tween needs to be understood as a distinct individual with tremendous variance in development.

that he traveled to Jerusalem with Joseph and Mary, then tarried in the temple to discuss the scriptures.

Tweens are much like adolescents, as their biggest needs may be structure and more adult involvement in their lives, not less structure and less adult (parental) involvement. However, they are unlike adolescents as tweens are not ready yet to deal with the freedom that will come with adolescence. They need constant reassurance that adults still care and are in touch with them. Free time activities are not of much help. They need guidance for how to spend that time.

> Tweens are not ready yet to deal with the freedom that will come with adolescence.

Physical Issues

Tweens come in all shapes, sizes, styles and differing developmental phases. Since the physical changes in this age group are so diverse and take place at such different times for individual tweens, it is difficult to speak of a typical or normal tween. When we do, we refer to the average, or median, range. While most tweens will have similar pathways of development, they will almost always differ in the times and ways they develop along those pathways. All tweens will face common physical changes during puberty, but when these occur and how they affect individual tweens will vary. Tweens will often demonstrate distinctive self-adaptive behavior to these physical changes. Physically, as well as emotionally and socially, some tweens will be firmly established in pubertal changes, while others will be in the various stages of preadolescence.

Skeletal and Muscular

During these years most tweens will grow an average of two to three inches a year. Muscle mass and strength gradually increase. Legs will lengthen and trunks will slim down as baby fat decreases. Growth is usually slow and consistent. Usually a child's body weight will double sometime during the tween years or just before the tween years, if they physically develop earlier than most. Tweens should exert considerable energy as they engage in different motor activities. To support their growth and active lives they need to consume more food than they did in early childhood; however, this is also the time that early signs of obesity and other food related illness can begin to appear or be a concern. Good examples of healthy eating and nutrition are a must. Sugar- and caffeine-laden foods ought to be avoided, even if we are used to them and find them more convenient. Teachers and adult leaders need to help provide these healthier alternatives rather than taking tweens to the closest fast food restaurants or offering snacks with questionable nutritional value.

> Good examples of healthy eating and nutrition are a must.

Puberty

Puberty is a period of rapid skeletal and sexual maturation that occurs mainly in early adolescence. For males, testosterone plays an important role, as does estrogen in females. This growth spurt occurs two years later for boys than girls—usually between ages twelve and thirteen for boys and ten to eleven for girls. Thus, all the issues of puberty can be significant for tweens, especially for girls since most of them will be in the midst of the most significant puberty development during this time frame. Studies consistently show that early maturing girls face a number of emotional problems that are not faced by slower developing females or males. A teacher or leader who understands these issues is especially welcome so that they can spend a moment or two with girls who face early puberty development issues.

Motor Skills

Motor development becomes smoother and more coordinated for most tweens. They gain greater control over their bodies and can sit still for longer periods of time. However, their lives should be activity-oriented and very active. While they can focus their energies for longer periods of time than younger children, teachers ought to avoid passive activities in teaching whenever possible. Substitute action activities, even in Sunday School, whenever possible in teaching. We will say more about this in another chapter.

While television and video games have gained in popularity and may seem like easy solutions to planning and teaching lessons, tweens need physical activity and movement to help them learn. Additionally, there is every indication that our children are not getting enough exercise at this age, so get them up and moving. This may even mean changing rooms so that physical activity is possible and not bothersome to other classes. Introducing a variety of games from other cultures and countries that one normally would not see on television or participate in at school can be very useful at this time.

> ## Teachers ought to avoid passive activities in teaching whenever possible.

It is our contention that sports, which can have a tremendously positive affect on the lives of tweens, can also have an extremely negative impact. On the positive side, structured sports can provide exercise, opportunities to learn how to compete, practice in fairness, increased self-esteem, and a setting to develop peer relations and friendships. On the negative side, sports can create too much pressure to achieve and win at any cost, cause physical injuries that can have lifelong consequences, distract from academic work, build unrealistic expectations of success as an athlete, and lead to the labeling of one as a "starter and winner" or as a "bench warmer and loser." We believe it is better for tweens to be involved in physical activity without the "premature structuring" (to borrow a phrase from David Elkind, author of *The Hurried Child*) that is predominant in so much of American athletic life. We also believe that this time of life is a perfect time to try new physical activities and sports without the risk of having to excel at them. While we will continually emphasize the need for tweens to be physically active, this should not be understood that they must become part of a team or be playing in leagues. Rather, tweens ought to enjoy the opportunity to grow in their motor skills and coordination through active involvement in life without the pressure or structure of leagues. There will be time enough for that in high school.

Stress

Stress can be understood as the response of individuals to the circumstances and events of life that threaten them and tax their coping abilities. Unfortunately, our culture seems to have created a more "stressful" world for tweens. While there is stress at every age and stage in life, we see more and more tweens struggling to cope with stress in their lives. While avoiding stress can be a short-term technique for tweens, through denial, regression, and impulsive acting out behavior, this is an important time to help tweens accept the fact that facing stress can be beneficial.

Learning and practicing different stress coping techniques such as humor and altruism can give tweens a way to work through life's pressures and issues. Certainly parents can also help remove those stressors that they can. In teaching, especially in the church community's role, we would hope that creating more stress in a tween's life is not your intended or unintended goal. We hope that the faith community and the classroom can become a safe environment where some of life's stressors can be discussed and dealt with in a faithful manner.

> Learning and practicing different stress coping techniques such as humor and altruism can give tweens a way to work through life's pressures and issues.

Stress Changes the Brain

Imaginary or real fears affect tweens. They often cannot tell the difference between real and remote threats, and both threats act the same way in the brain. Kids live with many of the same fears that adults do—divorce, separation from parents and/or friends, money, performance anxiety, abandonment, world violence, overextension, and violence—just to name a few. As resilient as girls and boys can be, stress physically affects the brain, which affects their behaviors.

Avoidance behaviors such as absenteeism are common; so are stomachaches and headaches, even nausea. It can go as far as depression. Girls especially are known for pouting. Think temper tantrum for older kids. Pouting is a learned behavior that likely worked for kids to get their way when they were younger. Boys and girls need time to deal with stress's precipitating causes in an appropriate manner. Physical activity to get their big muscles moving can help, as can having someone care enough to take time to listen to their concerns.

It takes time and practice to develop alternative ways of dealing with stress and learn how to manage it for persons of any age, and most tweens have not had enough practice; they haven't lived long enough to get it. They do not have the cognitive or psychosocial maturity to deal with stress well. It's up to the adults, especially the "SROs" in their lives, to help. SRO was a phrase that Dr. Dick Murray used often in his classes and conversations. SROs are the Significant Respected Others in our lives, those people whom we trust to tell us the truth and support us no matter what.

Your alert and attentive ears and eyes can help prevent or respond to tween stress. Watch for behaviors that you don't think are normal for that child. That means that you have to know what's normal for them. It's not always clear, so establish a habit of checking in with them with open-ended questions. Watch for signs of depression such as persistent sadness, hopelessness, diminished interest in friends and activities, low energy and low self-esteem, obsession with death, and suicidal talk. Consult with parents if you have concerns. Don't ignore or "stuff" any concerns you have.

Acknowledge and validate tweens' feelings. Minimalizing them won't make the feelings go away, but it might make the kids go away and not come back. Respond carefully. Share the amount and type of information that they need at the moment. Share facts as frankly and simply as you can. However, be careful in your sharing that this is not seen as correction in front of their peers.

> ## Acknowledge and validate tweens' feelings.

Pay attention to your own behaviors.

Pay attention to your own behaviors. "Mrs. Meyers, why do people act as if we have two heads?" asked a twelve year old. Patty's immediate reply was, "Because sometimes you act as if you have two heads," followed by a more serious response. She acknowledged that she heard what the person said, injected a little humor, then followed with information to help younger and older persons build bridges to each other.

Do things that relate to their concerns. Take positive action about things related to their concerns, such as working on a Heifer Project or care packages for children or shut-ins.

Ask if it is ok to give the tween a hug. Don't assume that it is. In the litigious age in which we live, an uninvited hug might upset a child and/or parent.

Do things that relate to their concerns.

Ask if they would like you to pray with or for them. Ask if they would like to pray. You can pray for them when they aren't around, but prayer can help upset girls and boys to calm down and center their energies toward getting the help that they need.

Remember that cynicism and anger are often masks for anxiety or fear. Remember, too, that emotions are not right or wrong; emotions are gifts from God. It's what we do with them that is either positive or negative. It is all right to be angry or afraid, but try to find out the cause of the anger or fear.

The very nature of being a tween, with all the inherent changes, is enough to cause stress. Since change is the name of the game for tweens and change is stressful, expect to deal with its effects on the tweens you know. Stress is a "hidden or null curriculum" whenever you work with tweens (*Fashion Me a People* by Maria Harris; Westminster John Knox Press, 1989; p. 69). Calm, consistent care and good modeling can help tweens work through or live with the causes of stress.

Summary

► Expect lots of physical changes in tweens

► Set and encourage good nutrition patterns

► Pay careful attention to both stress and issues of puberty

► Plan for and use physical activities as much as possible in the classroom

Chapter Two
COGNITIVE DEVELOPMENT

Tweens are dealing with intellectual changes. Some will begin to focus (perhaps too much) on academics in a desire to be the next Einstein or to get into Duke or Stanford. Others will begin to lose focus and devalue learning, often focusing on some other cultural form of hero, such as an athlete, rock star, X games contestant, or model. This is a time for balance in perspective and education. Despite what some might think, tweens' grades are not going to affect whether they get into Princeton. Rather, they are building an educational foundation that can be expanded throughout adolescence. However, as many in our culture prize intellectual competence and achievement, tweens can begin to feel the pressure to display intellectual achievement, which creates unbelievable stress in some. While encouraging tweens' natural intellectual and learning curiosity, we must not add to their stress with unrealistic expectations around memorizing long or large portions of the Bible or catechisms.

We will probably always be indebted to Jean Piaget for his theory of cognitive development. Piaget described four general periods of cognitive development:

> We must not add to their stress with unrealistic expectations around memorizing long or large portions of the Bible or catechisms.

1) sensory-motor, which occurs roughly from birth to two years of age;

2) pre-operational thought, which occurs between the ages of two and seven years;

3) concrete operations, which usually develop between the ages of seven and eleven;

4) formal operations, which usually does not begin until age 12 and continues developing through adulthood.

There are some who have built on Piaget's work to suggest a fifth stage of abstract thinking, and others believe that not all adults ever enter formal operations and may get stuck in concrete operational thought.

Most tweens are in concrete operations; that is, they develop the capacity to think systematically, but can only think in real, concrete terms, and not symbolically. For example, a cookie is a cookie. It doesn't represent the ingredients of a system that work together to create a new thing. What you see is what you get in concrete operations.

Older tweens may begin formal operations around age 12. This means they begin to develop the ability to think systematically and on purely abstract and hypothetical planes, yet they may not have the experience to further explore this new ability to think formally. This ability usually grows throughout our lifetimes, but most tweens do not yet possess the developmental ability to think like adults. Their brains are not yet that developed.

This is why we should not think of tweens as little adults, nor expect them to draw what we consider logical conclusions from material such as the Bible, nor make grown-up decisions. Tweens will draw conclusions from biblical stories, but what they focus on may not be as mature as what we expect, and perhaps not what the biblical narrative intends. Obviously we must be careful here, as the biblical narrative may have a number of levels of meaning, not just our meaning. Nonetheless, tweens still don't have the cognitive ability to think abstractly about the biblical narrative.

> Tweens still don't have the cognitive ability to think abstractly about the biblical narrative.

A few older tweens, closer to their teen years, may begin to discern the difference between the positive and negative and may see some alternatives to various issues (and not just black and white). They may begin to see the gray area between black and white, but even if they do, little of this gets applied, as it will take time for the adolescent brain to grow and expand. You cannot force cognitive thinking to grow at a faster rate.

Most tweens are still in what Piaget called concrete operational thought.

David Elkind describes three things that may be most helpful to us as teachers and parents about concrete operational thought. The tweens' minds are not blank slates. They have a host of ideas about the physical and natural world as well as life. These ideas differ from those of adults. We must learn to comprehend what tweens are saying and try to respond in the same mode of discourse that they intend to use, keeping in mind that tweens often sound street smart, parroting what they hear without fully knowing what they're saying.

Second, tweens are in a constant process of unlearning and relearning in addition to acquiring new knowledge and making sense of new experience. We can help this process by trying to present things in a way that may make sense to concrete operational thinkers. Again, we must be careful that in presenting things concretely we don't allow for the possibility that as the brain develops these concrete ideas become fixed and are not allowed to be learned again at a different cognitive level as tweens mature. For example, some have argued that many people, in thinking about the Bible or faith issues, have never moved past concrete operational thought, that the issues of how to interpret the Bible or how to think about one's faith become fixated at a concrete level. In this way, abstract thinking does not occur about the Bible and faith issues in the same way that it may about the nature of the universe. Others have argued that Piaget was mistaken in assuming that most people will reach the next stage of cognitive development, formal operational thought, and that some people never reach any form of abstract or formal thinking. In fact, some have argued that this is why children's sermons that focus on concrete issues, often with a concrete object, may be well received by adults, as they do not want to or cannot think abstractly about their faith.

> Tweens often sound street smart, parroting what they hear without fully knowing what they're saying.

Third, tweens by nature are motivated to acquire knowledge. The best way to nurture this motivation for knowledge is to let them interact with the environment. Thus we need to protect against an overly rigid curriculum that disrupts the tweens' own pace of learning and interest. However, educators debate this point too. In today's educational climate, it is not fashionable to allow tweens some sense of pace in their own learning process. Our culture and government have started requiring strict tests to gauge whether tweens are learning what we want them to learn.

Others will debate whether tweens are that motivated to learn. We would argue that tweens are self-motivated. If your tweens are not that motivated, you may need to change your teaching style to tap into their natural curiosity and interest. While popular today, we do not believe that an overly rigid teaching style or an overly rigid curriculum that does not allow tweens to move where their interests develop is helpful in the long run in getting tweens to learn. Their pace and answers to questions they have about God and the faith may not be the questions that we adults have for them.

Most, if not all, tweens lack the reflective ability for philosophical questioning. For most tweens, faith is commonly a matter of following rules and living up to authority figure expectations (usually their parents', but could be teachers' and/or a pastor's). However, they are beginning to tire of the rules and have not yet developed the cognitive thinking skills to view religion intuitively. It is a time to patiently listen to their questions

> It is a time to develop friendships and relationships that, over time, can become safe places where faith issues are discussed.

and doubts (remember Thomas the disciple; Jesus allowed the doubting one to be part of the inner circle his entire ministry despite Thomas's doubts). It is a time to develop friendships and relationships that, over time, can become safe places where faith issues are discussed, especially as tweens move into being adolescents. It is a time when your actions and your faith responses may speak louder than any lesson or words. Lecturing is not usually very helpful, but providing case studies and "what if" situations may spur their thinking and their interest. We address teaching strategies more fully in chapter six and faith formation issues in chapter five.

Tweens are beginning to develop critical thinking skills. That means that they are grasping the deeper meaning of problems, beginning to keep open minds about different approaches and perspectives, and thinking reflectively rather than accepting statements and carrying out teachers' and parents' directions without significant understanding and evaluation. The answer "because I said so" to a tween's question or issue is not usually a helpful response during this developmental period. The tween, who may seem to be just defying authority, is probably asking for help in understanding your reasoning and may actually want a conversation about your reasoning since it does not make sense to them with their limited experience and concrete thinking. But again, taking the time to explain your rationale does not mean the tween will understand it, let alone accept it. This is the time to help tweens begin, not complete, the process of developing problem solving strategies, of improving their knowledge base and becoming motivated to use their newly developing thinking skills, especially around faith issues. Remember that tweens are not going to think about faith issues like you do as an adult.

For example, according to Robert Selman, tweens are developing the sense that both self and others can view each other, what he calls mutual perspective taking, but tweens are not yet ready to move into social and conventional perspective taking, where an adolescent realizes that just seeing one other person's point of view does not always lead to full understanding and that there are multiple perspectives, including social conventions (*The Growth of Interpersonal Understanding*; Academic Press, 1980).

Tweens are also improving greatly on their long-term memory skills. The issue of long-term memory development now allows several successive units to build upon themselves in Sunday school curriculum for the first time. Previously, you may have been able to build a unit or two upon each other, but long-term memory development was insufficient to sustain the memory of the important

> Long-term memory development now allows several successive units to build upon themselves in Sunday school curriculum for the first time.

issues for very long. For example, we might be able to do a cute children's sermon on the "Tater family" where different potatoes are dressed as different "-taters"—hesitator, dictator, imitator—and you may find your children playing with your potatoes, but they are rarely able to remember the concepts behind the names beyond a week or two. Now, tweens are able to remember the names and the concepts if they work on developing their long term memory. Thus it may become appropriate to work on some memorization, if the point is not just to memorize a "Bible fact," but to help the tweens develop a biblical foundation that they can draw on later in life.

Computers

Computers have shaped American life in a new way. The shape of American life that computers have created is only now beginning to emerge and to be thought about in any type of critical way. Each successive generation in American life is shaped more and more by computers. Most tweens will be part of this computer literate generation. Among the potential positive effects of computers on tween development is the use of computer as a personal tutor, as a multipurpose tool and the motivational and social aspects of its use. Among the potential negative affects are the regimentation and dehumanization of the classroom and the limitations of social interaction through a computer.

Of course, with the computer has also come the Internet. We believe that no tween should have unlimited or unsupervised access to the Internet. The Internet, while providing an unparalleled instant access to information, also provides an unparalleled instant access to the evils of society and humankind. Further, the computer (especially games) and the various facets of media (especially television) have allowed tweens to focus less on the development of reading skills and the process of acquiring knowledge through reading than we believe is healthy for an educated and informed citizenry. Tweens need to learn how a library is used and to develop the skills of reading. All life's information is not going to be available in some techno-version by the time tweens reach adulthood. They will need to learn how to read and how to find information outside of the Internet.

> Planned, organized activities give tweens a forum for relating to each other.

CONCLUSION

Tweens need structured activities, groups of friends, a forum for questioning ideas and a rationale for learning at school or at the church. Planned, organized activities give tweens a forum for relating to each other (other than the punching, slapping, and hitting that is often just a way for tweens to try to connect when they don't know how or an imitation of the behavior of older teens they see in videos, movies, and other forms of media).

Organized sports (without focusing on teams and winning), music groups, formal hobbies, school clubs, and a variety of church-related activities provide organization for tweens to grow. Again, forced activities that tweens are not interested in or are not naturally inclined toward or activities which place a premium on achievement may limit the involvement of those who do not excel at those activities. These are not helpful organization plans for tweens.

Tweens do not always do well with too much free time, which can create boredom and a looking for excitement outside of the normal limits. Friendship groups can become extremely important as tweens band together for reinforcement. Parents and the church need to support gatherings of buddies by providing transportation, time, and a safe place to congregate. This is not the local mall! Besides the issue of safety and boredom, our consumer culture does not need tweens with credit cards shopping with their friends without parental supervision. They are not ready yet, even if they think they are! Some tweens have serious questions and real concerns. You need to take the time to really listen to them and to their responses.

SUMMARY

▶ Tweens are not little adults; their cognitive development is not that far along yet

▶ Tweens need organized activities and groups with supervision, not free time

▶ Tweens need opportunities to engage in activities that have and hold their interests, not our interests as adults

▶ Tweens need adults who really listen and try to understand their reasoning while pointing tweens to other reasons beyond their thinking

▶ Tweens are ready to begin (and it is just a beginning) building a biblical and theological foundation in remembering the stories of the biblical narrative, but they will interpret the narratives differently

Chapter Three
SOCIO-EMOTIONAL DEVELOPMENT

Many tweens have vast internal emotional changes happening that they don't quite understand. For many, especially girls, puberty hits with the force of a hurricane. These emotional changes may manifest themselves in increased frustration with parents, growing concern to look attractive to the opposite sex, or a desire to be involved in activities with the opposite sex. There may be a preoccupation with sexual excitement. They can become resentful of parental authority and especially of parental rules that impinge on their growing social awareness. They can turn to pornography or older teens and especially the imitation of older teen behavior. This is an important time for sex education, but with a clear understanding of sex that goes well beyond the plumbing involved. This is the time to focus on sexual limits and on understanding feelings. This is not the time to address the gray areas of ethics, as tweens are not prepared, nor do they have the brain development, to grasp these subtle questions and deal with them as adults or older adolescents do.

Tweens are undergoing vast social changes. Some will feel this effect much more than others. Some will fret and worry all the time about who likes them and if they are in the right group while others could care less about others' opinions of them. Social groups tend to fluctuate and can be reconstituted rather quickly for some and not for others. Many tweens express loneliness, fear, frustration, or isolation, and much of this can be linked to the socio-emotional changes which they experience. Several of the gun-packing students in the school shootings that got so much press attention in the 1990's were tweens. Tweens need clear rules and close (preferably parental) supervision as they head toward the even more topsy-turvy world of adolescent friendships.

> Tweens need clear rules and close... supervision.

Cultural changes that seem to happen at the speed of light in our times add to this already volatile transition period for tweens. The changing nature of parent-child relationships, stepfamilies, latchkey tweens, and peer popularity, rejection, or neglect are just a few of the changes with which tweens and those who care for them must cope.

Tweens can be either loquacious or laconic. You can never predict which they will be. It is amazing how the eight or nine year old chatterboxes can become the quiet, pensive, keep-it-to-myself twelve year olds. It is equally amazing how these same tweens can slide from one to the other within just a very short time span as puberty crashes in on them.

Dealing with Change

The concept of transition and change started when Adam and Eve left the Garden of Eden. Change can be as difficult for a ten year old as it is for someone thirty or forty or sixty. We cringe when we hear someone tell a child, "You don't know anything about problems. Just wait until you're our age." Tween problems are just as great to them as adults consider their own problems to be, and tweens have far few life experiences and resources to deal with life's struggles than adults do.

> Tween problems are just as great to them as adults consider their own problems to be.

> It is easier to keep values and beliefs . . . than to try to reclaim them.

Tweens are kids struggling between "Don't you see I need help?" and "Leave me alone and let me do it by myself." This is a time of transition from almost total acceptance of parental values to the growing challenge of peer pressure and questioning of those parental and church values. Change is inevitable!

Emphasis on the glamour and urgency of growing up has been pushed from the teen years to the tweens. Fashion houses now design and market clothes especially for the 9-12 age group. Parents and the church leaders must tailor their activities and programs to offset the bombardment of the media and other secular influences. It is easier to keep values and beliefs through the tween years than to try to reclaim them when they are teenagers. In other words, help them get it right from the beginning because it is much harder to change behavior after they have learned something the wrong way.

Parent—Tween Relationships

Children who receive inadequate attention during the tween years may be much more difficult to shepherd during the adolescent years. Thus it is important that parents and the church spend time building relationships with tweens and listening to their concerns.

Parents often spend less time with tweens than they previously did since much of childhood's caregiving, instruction, reading, talking, and playing is over. Still, parents are powerful and important socializing agents during this period. They must maintain their connection and support of their tween or they could face some really dangerous waters ahead.

> It is important that parents and the church spend time building relationships with tweens and listening to their concerns.

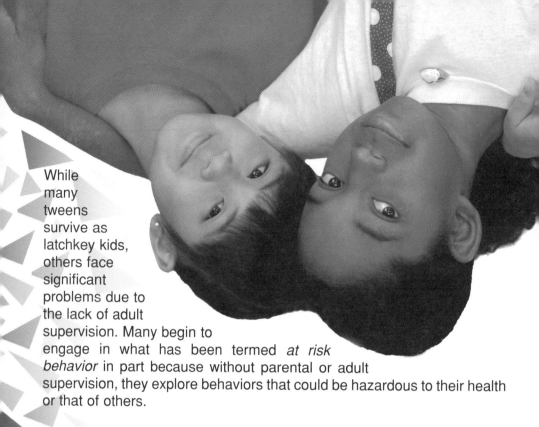

While many tweens survive as latchkey kids, others face significant problems due to the lack of adult supervision. Many begin to engage in what has been termed *at risk behavior* in part because without parental or adult supervision, they explore behaviors that could be hazardous to their health or that of others.

The changing nature of families can be very stressful, especially during the tween years. Many tweens are members of single parent or stepfamilies. Usually, during this period discipline needs to change and control ought to be more coregulatory. This area gets even more muddied when another adult merges into the picture and authority issues bubble up.

Generally, girls have a more difficult time accepting a stepmom than boys do. Over time, tween boys seem to improve in acceptance and dealing with a stepdad more than girls do, and in time, they certainly do better at the initial introduction of a stepparent during this emotional time of life. Rivalry for attention and special recognition in the family is often problematic, as parents may not communicate with each other or with their tween. Fair and equitable treatment of all members of the family can generally ease any tensions. However, if significant problems occur, extended conversations with helping professionals trained in dealing with tween and family issues are recommended.

While some in our culture have suggested that people ought to have to take out a license to have children—thus enabling parenting classes to be taught as a precondition of the granting of a child rearing license—having children remains an individual choice.

Generally, parenting has been left to the biological parents unless the society believes a child is in danger; then the society has been willing to step in and remove or attempt to change a home situation. As a member of society and the Church, you are required by law to be alert and remain vigilant about potential child abuse. This issue has received much attention in the church lately and excellent resources are available. We especially recommend *Safe Sanctuaries: Reducing the Risk of Child Abuse in the Church*, by Joy T. Melton (Discipleship Resources, 1998). Melton is an attorney with expertise in this area and offers workshops with those who work with children and youth.

Generally speaking, there are four styles of parenting:

1) authoritarian, which is a restrictive and punitive style that focuses on a parent's authority and allows little if any tween response;

2) authoritative, which encourages a tween to start moving toward independence but still places limits and controls on the tween's actions;

3) permissive-indulgent, where parents are very involved in the life of the tween, but place few, if any restrictions on them; and

4) permissive-indifferent, where parents are not involved in a tween's life and tend to ignore the tween.

In this culture, which prizes independent but responsible adults, authoritative parenting is accepted as the most positive form of parenting. This style enables extensive give and take between the parents and the tweens. Parents are warm and nurturing toward their tween. Parents slowly allow tweens to take on more and more independence as they demonstrate more and more socially responsible behavior. If responsible behavior is not forthcoming, then stricter limits and parental controls are again enforced. Although consistent parenting is usually recommended, a wise parent may sense the importance of being more permissive in certain situations, more authoritarian in others, and yet more authoritative in others.

Usually parental authority will begin to be challenged during this time frame, especially by girls. Many males, with a later puberty development cycle, may not start challenging parental authority until early adolescence. The challenging of parental authority is normal, but is not to be confused with excessive defiance of authority. It is extremely important, in our view, that parents and teachers of tweens establish warm, trusting relationships that enable effective communication to occur. It's easier for everyone to get along when limits are placed on tween behavior with known consequences and the adults consistently employ the consequences. If parents and teachers do not take the time to be with tweens and help parent them toward adolescence and then adulthood, other environmental factors will do the parenting (such as peers and the media).

> It is extremely important that parents and teachers of tweens establish warm, trusting relationships that enable effective communication to occur.

Tween—Peer Friendships

Parents have more influence over tweens' choice and acceptance of peers than they think. The choice of school and church and sometimes even neighborhood can often influence greatly the peer choices for tweens. Whoever the tweens' peers are, tweens will spend an increasing amount of time with them. Most tween activity between peers is general play, going places, and socializing ("hanging out"). Generally, tweens spend more time with people of their gender than with tweens of the opposite sex. If an individual tween seems overly interested in opposite sex relationship, group activities are recommended over significant time alone with opposite sex friends or dating. Group dating is much preferred over individual dating during the tween years.

With the onset of puberty, peer pressure and conformity continue to play important roles in the tween years, especially older Tweens and especially among girls. We must remember that peer conformity is not always negative and can be a very positive influence in the lives of tweens. Peer conformity, especially with anti-social behavior, usually peaks at about ninth grade, but can begin during tween years. It can be seen as a signal that all is not right with the tween development.

Peer group relationships are usually of the crowd, clique, or individual friendship variety. Crowds usually focus on common interests. This is where church programming can be beneficial, giving tweens an opportunity to gather around common interests in a safe, inviting environment. Cliques are smaller but have greater cohesion and involve greater intimacy among tweens. Cliques can be beneficial as tweens begin to establish their identity, but they also can limit friendships and have tremendously negative impact on tween self esteem.

> Church programming can be beneficial, giving tweens an opportunity to gather around common interests in a safe, inviting envirionment.

Parents and teachers ought to take an active interest in the development of peer relationships. They should know who relates well to whom and why. They ought to ask questions about the relationships and understand the dynamics of the relationships. We recommend that tweens not spend extended time activities without adult supervision. We do not believe tweens ought to spend hours in a mall shopping with credit cards and without adult supervision. Most tweens aren't ready developmentally for all that peer relationships involve, even if they think they are. Tweens need help making responsible decisions (not overly influenced by their peers or impulse related decisions). They need to understand the decision-making process, which adults can model and demonstrate.

> **Tweens need help making responsible decisions.**

With parents often spending less time with tweens, peer friendships become much more important. While we understand the pressures with which parents struggle, it is still important for parents to monitor the nature and depth of those peer relationships. According to one researcher, tween friendships serve six functions: companionship, ego support, social comparison, physical support, stimulation, and intimacy/affection (*Conversations of Friends*, J. M. Gottman and J. G. Parker, eds.; Cambridge University Press, 1987). These six functions can be healthy or not, depending on the degree to which they meet tweens' socio-emotional needs.

For some tweens, media plays the role of supervisor when other adult supervision or peer friendships are not available. The images available through the media can greatly affect the tween. As some have said, the issue is not if there will be parenting done, but who will parent the tween? The media, peers or parents? We will address this issue more fully in the next chapter.

> **Often this is a period of time when gender stereotypes are reinforced.**

Gender Issues

Often this is a period of time when gender stereotypes are reinforced.

38

Some researchers believe that many of the differences between males and females have been previously exaggerated. Others point to the specific social context the tween inhabits as the main force in gender issues. Certainly in today's American culture, particularly among some males, problem behaviors such as drug use (especially alcohol), delinquency, and school problems are associated with their beliefs surrounding gender identity or masculinity.

This is the time to begin to help both girls and boys understand the imbalance or balance of power between males and females (this is particularly relevant around sexual issues). While girls at this age may be as physically imposing or even more imposing than some boys, this balance of power will not last. The attention given to female athletes in the past two decades may have actually hindered the development of understanding the imbalance of power between men and women, physically and in other ways.

Puberty

Puberty is a period of rapid skeletal change and sexual maturation that occurs in many tweens, although some will wait until early adolescence to go through these changes. Puberty has been occurring at increasingly earlier ages. For example, the average age of first menstruation in this country is a year earlier than in most European countries, at approximately age twelve and a half years. In 1840 it was about age 17, and in 1900 at about fourteen and a half years (see "Secular Trends in Human Growth Maturation and Development" by A. F. Roche, *Monographs of the Society for Research in Child Development*, #179, 44:20).

While the reasons for this earlier menstruation don't seem clear, we realize that tweens are entering puberty at earlier ages than many of today's adults did. Since a number of physical changes occur, it is difficult to point to one event to say that puberty is started, finished, or has occurred. Additionally, puberty is not an environmental accident. Genetics, nutrition, health, and body mass all play a role in human physical development.

Recent research suggests that being an early developing male is more advantageous than being a late developing one, but early maturation for girls can be a significant problem. Still, most tweens will weather puberty's challenges competently. Unfortunately, adults often wait too long to broach the subject of sex and other issues that puberty creates. Tweens don't wait and when appropriate adults are not readily available with information and education, they get that education and information, such as it is, from peers and media.

> **Adults often wait too long to broach the subject of sex and other issues that puberty creates.**

Sexuality

Psychotherapist Linda S. Mintle, Ph. D., writes: "The sexual content in magazines marketed to tweens bombards them with graphic images and ideas. At a time when they struggle to understand their sexual development and are undecided about sexual choices, these magazines encourage readers to act out their impulses. They expose tweens to sexual messages prior to their emotional readiness to handle them. For example, Cosmopolitan Girl, 'a cool magazine for teens,' tells girls how to give "an absolutely heavenly New Year's Eve kiss." The guidelines are graphic and erotic. An advertisement for a Maidenform bra reads, 'Inner beauty only goes so far.' Cosmetic Surgery magazine provides 98 pages of ways to improve your looks. Teens are now one of the fastest growing plastic surgery markets. What's the message to budding pubescent girls? The media messages are provocative and ignoble, offering graphic guidelines for inappropriate behaviors to tweens.

"Take a look at the magazines marketed to children. Read the articles and discuss the appropriateness of the sexual content. Sit with tweens and ask if this is helping them develop self-control and an acceptable view of their bodies. Then, discuss God's emphasis on the heart and character.

> **Discuss God's emphasis on the heart and character.**

"In an oversexed culture, it's important to teach young girls balance between looking nice and obsessing on beauty as defined by that culture. Being obsessed with appearance often causes girls to develop eating problems. Tweens, especially girls, need to see who they are in Christ—wonderfully made, created in God's image, and more valuable than the sparrows. Girls don't need to be 'Cosmo Girls.' They need to be real girls, mirrored after the image of the heavenly maker, God."

It is our hope that the Olsen twins, current tween heroes, will remain as wholesome in their image as they have in the past and not follow the example that Christina Aguilera and Britney Spears set in marketing sexuality. Time will tell with these contemporary role models and with your tweens. Certainly there seems to be a preoccupation among some tweens with sex, physical contact, and experimentation at an early age.

Summary

In summary, tweens' bodies go through dramatic changes. Those physical changes impact their socio-emotional development and their relationships with parents, peers, and others. Simultaneously, they face a lot of pressure to grow up even faster in the fast-moving culture in which they live. It's not easy to be a tween. They can be badly hurt by unscrupulous people if not supported and supervised by loving adults. Here are some do's and don'ts, things that you can do to help tweens with their socio-emotional development:

▶ Do find time to listen to tween concerns over issues of sexuality and body image

▶ Don't encourage same sex or opposite sex relationships and dating

▶ Do encourage group activities

▶ Do watch for signs of abuse and report them

▶ Do expect lots of physical changes and concerns both positive and negative that come from these changes

▶ Do provide physical activity, although some girls farther along in puberty may not want to play what they now perceive as boy's or children's games

▶ Do expect some questioning of authority and listen, remembering that tweens do not yet think like you do!

▶ In all things, embrace change

Tweens will survive this turbulent time of life, but we want them to do more than survive. We hope that they thrive.

Chapter Four

CULTURAL ISSUES

Introduction

Four significant cultural expressions provide the primary influences on tweens in our opinion: parents or parental figures, peers, media, and school and the activities that tweens' schools sponsor or support. In the case of the tweens you will be working with, we may be able to add a fifth cultural influence, the Church! These institutions, while vastly different, remain the major influencers in the lives of tweens. In the previous chapter we spent some time talking about the parents and peer issues. In this chapter we want to focus on schools and media. You may feel out of place in this discussion, since you are "just" a teacher/leader or a parent, but you are advocates for tweens and you can make a difference in the way these cultural expressions affect the lives of tweens.

> You [the teachers] are the advocates for tweens and you can make a difference in the way these cultural expressions affect the lives of tweens.

Schools

Since mandatory schooling became the law of the land about 100 years ago, schools have assumed a larger and larger role in the development of all children in our culture. The emergence of junior high schools to help students make the transitions to high schools came about in part because of the recognition of the physical, social and cognitive changes that take place in the younger adolescent population. The junior school has now emerged as a middle school, where the focus has usually become the sixth through the eighth grade (although many other patterns exist due to issues of building size and rapidly changing student population size in any given year in an individual school system). This concept has met with a lot of support, given all the changes taking place in students in those years, including earlier puberty development.

However, the transition for tweens from elementary school to a middle school can be very stressful. With all the other changes going on in a tween's life, many of them do not need yet another stressor like changing schools. Additionally, the "top dog" phenomenon, where a tween moves from the top position in elementary school as the oldest and biggest to the lowest position as the youngest and smallest students in the school, concerns many researchers because it has created an overly negative view of school for the first year during the transition. Additionally, at-risk behavior dramatically increases in some tweens.

Currently, the issue of middle school is a hot topic. At present, there are a variety of research studies currently investigating ways to address these concerns as tweens make the transition to middle school. The possible suggestions for making the transition less stressful range from making schools smaller to keeping each grade level of a middle school isolated on separate wings of the

> The issue of middle school is a hot topic.

building. In her book *The War Against Excellence*, Cheri Pierson Yecke expresses her belief that middle school has become not an educational institution where children learn important skills and knowledge but a social engineering vehicle that attends endlessly to dogma and dreamy notions while teaching very little (Praeger, 2003). The concept of middle school, what needs to be taught, and how it should be taught will be addressed in the next few years across the country. There seems to be no general consensus at the present time about the direction of changes that will take place in the middle school concept. What does seem clear is that students with greater friendship contacts and a higher quality of friendships have better feelings about the transition to middle school and, in general, do better in the transition year.

Middle school is dramatically different for older tweens from the elementary school they previously attended. No longer top dogs, many of them struggle with the transition and have very negative feelings about school, teachers and their self-image. They seem to need a more

44

supportive environment and an opportunity to feel good about themselves now that they are the youngest and smallest again. Adding to their feelings of inadequacy is that school faculty and administrators often assume that they know how to change classes, how to keep things in a locker, how to make decisions about classes, and other things they are ill prepared to do at this stage of life.

Most parents, and indeed most of the population, trust that what is happening at school is good for their children. There seems to be an implicit trust that the administrators are doing what is best for each individual tween and for the culture. Unfortunately, this is not always the case. For example, a middle school administrator recently decided that parents could only get their children at 11 am during the school day (from a Mecklenburg County, North Carolina, school district bulletin). This change has been met with general acceptance rather than outrage challenging the policy, which has made the school a virtual prison for children where they have limited access to their parents.

We believe that parents, and you as teachers of tweens, ought to visit the schools tweens attend on a regular basis, observing and supporting the educational system wherever appropriate. However, we also believe that many questions need to be asked of individual schools, especially as questionable administrative or teaching decisions are made. After all, the school remains the biggest potential influencer in the lives of our children; it is estimated that they spend over 10,000 forced hours as members of a small society in which tasks are to be accomplished and tweens socialized with particular rules that define behavior.

We also believe that it is beneficial for tweens to develop hobbies (although some parents have gone overboard with too many hobbies) during this stage of life. Adolescents need to have at least one thing on which they can focus and feel competence or mastery of outside of the classroom. For some this may be athletics or church or music, but the development of some sort of worthwhile hobby will help tremendously during adolescence. One of Ed's foster children used to say that God had given him a gift as a pickpocket, so why shouldn't he use the gift? Ed would gently and then not so gently remind him that pickpocketing is not a gift from God, nor is it socially acceptable behavior. Hobbies ought to be socially acceptable and not increase at-risk behavior.

Media

One of the most pervasive influences of modern American life is the media. We have the opportunity to limit the pervasiveness of the media message, but only if we take the time to limit access to the media and to help tweens appraise the media message that is being delivered. We highly recommend the very readable

> Patiently make yourself available...for regular communication.

and informative book *Winning Your Kids Back From the Media* by Quentin J. Schultze (Intervarsity Press, 1994.) Most parenting books that deal with the media have one universal message: patiently make yourself available, whether you are a teacher or a parent, for regular communication, especially listening to your tween.

One cannot make sense of the media or help your tween make sense of it if you have no idea what they are consuming in terms of the media. Certainly we cannot isolate tweens from media, but we cannot simply ignore the media either. As parents (and to a lesser degree, as teachers), you have the role and responsibility to limit the access to various forms of media (for example, no Internet, phone or television in a tween bedroom where adult supervision is unavailable). As teachers, you can and ought to ask probing questions about the forms of media being used. Violent music may not create violent behavior, but it certainly signals that something may be occurring in a tween that could be cause for concern.

> We, as the church, as parents, and as concerned adults working with tweens, need to raise their awareness about issues of image.

The magazines that are directed to girls present unbelievably poor role images and models. The focus is almost exclusively on sex and image (and many of these magazines are run and produced by women, so it is not a male thing). Males tend to consume very specific forms of magazines directed at a particular activity such as skate boarding, but these too have incredibly poor models for males. We, as the church, as parents, and as concerned adults working with tweens, need to raise their awareness about issues of image (particularly body image) health and sexuality. Excessive use of the Internet, chat rooms, and video games may also signal a disruption of the emotional balance of a tween. Gentle questioning of the tween to probe what is going on lets them know that you care about every aspect of life.

Mass media is a tremendous vehicle for communication that, fundamentally, is in the identity-shaping business. The media creates and/or reflects the basic values and beliefs of the people who use it. As a major purveyor of identity-building in our world, the media needs our input about the kind of values we want our kids to have. That is why it is essential that we of the church, parents and teachers, must hold strong stances to help tweens interact, understand and disseminate the identity being created and be proactive about influencing the media that comes into our homes and other institutions.

Using Media

On a brighter note, the use of media can enhance teaching, especially if we are sensitive to the needs of the tweens. Music, video, Internet, computers, and news stories can all help enhance the teaching experience. Media ought not to take the place of good teacher/student interaction, nor should it ever be used without ample time to debrief. Extensive use of out-of-date media should be discouraged, since it will only demonstrate that you, as a teacher, are out of date, and thus have no worthwhile message for these media-savvy tweens.

> Media ought not take the place of good teacher/student interaction, nor should it be used without ample time to debrief.

For better and for worse, the media is here to stay, but it is up to us how we allow it to change and shape our identity and the identity of individuals with whom we have contact. Tweens are highly impressionable and they need our guidance as they forge their identities.

Summary

Peers, parents, media, and the school are the biggest influences on tween life. These four shape the environment and the development of a tween. Care must be taken to use these influencers in a positive way and to limit the potentially destructive nature of their role. The following list recaps what you can do to work with the cultural influences on tweens:

► Visit the school regularly

► Develop good parenting strategies

► Watch for signs of child abuse and report them

► Take interest in peer relationships

► Limit opposite sex relationships

► Supervise media use

► Take time to listen

► Always care and express God's love.

Don't be defeated by all the cultural issues in tweens' lives. Work with these four (or five) major influences to help them successfully navigate their way through them.

Chapter Five
FAITH DEVELOPMENT

Introduction

Helping people grow in their faith is one of the church's most important tasks. It is also one of the most challenging and enjoyable things that we do. How do we do it? It helps to know where to start. This chapter introduces you to some basic theory about faith development and describes the stages of faith that tweens are usually in at this time of their lives. These descriptions will help you know how to relate to them personally and how to make good choices for learning opportunities to help them develop in their relationships with God, themselves and others.

Most tweens lack the ability for abstract and formal thinking, thus religion tends to be simply accepting their parent's faith, that is, they try to live up to the rules and regulations of that faith as presented to them. When tweens become resentful of the rules they may focus not on the abstract concepts of their parents' faith, but on how church makes them feel (most of them want some sort of emotional high). Often they find their parent's faith lacking in creating the feeling that they want to experience, and so they resist the rules or the traditions that they see as not allowing their feelings.

> Most of them [tweens] want some sort of emotional high.

Tweens embody the stuff of faith, including its flipside, doubt. They are infinitely curious about life. They ask challenging questions and will tackle any task that captures their imaginations. They experience anguishing disappointments and jubilant victories, often one right after the other on the roller coaster of life, because most have not learned the concept or mastered the skill of postponing dealing with their feelings, nor do they yet have a reservoir of life experiences in which to place these emotions within a context.

While the definition of faith is debated, faith is not normally understood as unconditional acceptance of or compliance to a set of doctrines. We can believe in doctrines, yet faith is no more the result of these doctrines than the color of a person's eyes is the result of their favorite stories. Faith is a way of knowing and being in relation with God, or what theologian Paul Tillich called "the ultimate ground of our being." We reveal our faith in the way that we act and the decisions that we make. It has been said that faith is more "caught than taught," which implies that a lot of what teachers and leaders do is to provide situations and opportunities so that people will be in

> # We reveal our faith in the way that we act and the decisions that we make.

prime spaces to catch and grow in their faith. Others may insist that faith is a gift given by God. Rick Osmer describes faith as a cube with four to six sides of which not all are visible at the same time. (*Teaching for Faith*, Westminster John Knox, 1992)

After introducing theories that help us understand what tweens are like, this chapter will help teachers and leaders know what they can do to help them grow in their faith. Some specific suggestions will help you get going with these special young people.

THEORY: WHERE TWEENS ARE IN THEIR FAITH DEVELOPMENT

The designation tween is a clue that we cannot pigeonhole these people, nor should we try. Theories help us to understand and accept people where they are. Tweens don't consider themselves children anymore and they aren't adolescents yet; they are transitioning between stages, including stages of faith. Several scholars and researchers have contributed to our understanding of how people mature in their faith and the predictable stages in which they progress. Among them are James W. Fowler, John Westerhoff, Mary Wilcox, Anne Gilbert, Scott McLennan, and Delia Halverson. Combining their work and our own observations, we offer the following descriptions of the most likely stages in which tweens will be.

The **MYTHIC-LITERAL** stage is also called the Affiliative, Literalist or Reality stage. It usually describes people in the elementary to middle school years, between the ages of six and twelve. It describes many tweens, teens, and some adults.

Description of the stage: People in this stage begin to take on for themselves the stories, beliefs, and observances that symbolize belonging to their communities, whether the community is a town, school, class, sports team, a hand bell choir, Scouts, their families or any other group. If they have been raised in a home where religion is valued, they likely have a strong sense of authority and religious tradition. Even people who are not raised in religious households develop some sense of authority and religious tradition depending on the culture.

They interpret their beliefs literally, and their beliefs are infused with moral rules and attitudes. They are just approaching formal operations cognitively; most are still in concrete operations. That means that they are just beginning to make sense of symbols. They often understand symbols literally, as having only one dimension rather than several possibilities. They don't understand that symbols are metaphors that point to other realities. They organize the world in concrete terms. Their image of God is anthropomorphic, that is, human. For example, they may picture God as a white-bearded grandfather or as a loving, generous grandmother in the sky. Their world centers on themselves and they hold that world together with stories they have heard in their families and communities.

> It is important that everyone have ample opportunities to succeed.

Tweens often have a linear, narrative outlook on life. While they have an increasing ability to take others' perspectives, their empathy is limited. They understand the Golden Rule as "Do to others as they do to you" (see chart, *Understanding Faith Development*, by Mary Wilcox, 1986). What happens to and with them at this time of life can lead to self-affirmation or to feelings of inferiority, so it is important that everyone have ample opportunities to succeed.

Strengths of the stage: As previously noted, people in this stage have increasing narrative abilities. Their abilities to understand and show compassion increase with time and practice over previous stages. Their capacity for storytelling and reaching out to others can be quite remarkable.

Possible dangers of the stage: Because they take things so literally, people in this stage sometimes develop a stilted perfectionism, which shows in their thinking that there is only one right way to do things. They don't differentiate between fact and fiction very well; they accept things at face value. Another danger is a kind of works righteousness ("I'm good because I do good things and get praise"). Another possible danger is an abasing sense of badness ("I must be really bad to cause terrible thing to happen") if they have experienced mistreatment, abuse, neglect, or the disfavor of significant others in their lives.

There is a simplicity and security in this stage. For some, it provides a basis for a lifetime of deep conviction and commitment from which they may not further develop. Held together by stories, they know what they believe, and they aren't bothered by different interpretations. They are growing in their acceptance and affiliation with a group, and that's good enough for them. For others it is a starting point for new explorations of faith that may continue throughout their lives.

Transition to the next stage: As with any kind of growth, transition to the next stage happens when the old stage no longer fits, much as a foot outgrows size two shoes and requires size three shoes in order to relieve the growing pains. The faith development transition happens when clashes between stories and viewpoints must be faced and some reflective thought becomes possible. Previous literalism breaks down as they become more open to new ideas and develop perspectives that require more personal relationships with the unifying power and the questions they ask can no longer be satisfied with literal answers. Stage two no longer fits and causes growing pains, from which they seek relief, thus bringing a transition to another stage of faith development.

SYNTHETIC-CONVENTIONAL FAITH is sometimes called the Loyalist, Conformist or Dependence stage. It usually occurs sometime after age twelve. This stage continues the need to affiliate with some sort of community. This stage most often happens with youth, but also describes many adults. However, since people aren't made with cookie cutters, they may develop more quickly or slowly than others. Here is a brief description of the Synthetic-Conventional Faith Stage.

Description: This stage of faith is called conventional because people in it think that everyone's faith is the same. It is synthetic in that it is not analytical; it comes as a sort of unified, global whole with thoughts and feelings fused together. They accept truth if it feels right without examining it critically. Their life experience now reaches beyond the family. It's the gang stage; groups and peers are very important. People in this stage don't yet have a grasp of their own identity, so conformity and agreement are paramount as they locate authority outside themselves. A big part of the group's importance stems from its providing a sense of belonging, acceptance and identity.

While they hold beliefs deeply, they do so tacitly because they don't want to be different from the rest of their group. Persons in this stage need a strong sense of community with like-minded people. They empathize with people who are like them and are often ready and willing to help others who are like themselves or who are unfortunate. In this stage, most folks' faith is congruent with their own church, synagogue, friends, or whoever is in their most significant peer group.

For many, this stage adequately provides meaning for their lives. Interpersonal relationships take place, but clashes between various authorities inevitably occur. They control chaos by having and abiding by set rules from which no one may deviate. Their concept of God is that of awe and mystery. Their God is a judge who controls people in loving but exacting ways. They may not fully understand it, but they accept it. The majority of Americans are best described by this stage, especially as it deals with institutional authority.

Strengths of this stage: It incorporates the past and anticipated future in an image of ultimate environment. There is security and power in numbers. Many people do not develop beyond this stage. It feeds people's essential need to belong and be accepted. A majority of Americans do not develop beyond the synthetic-conventional stage of faith development.

Dangers of this stage: The expectations and evaluations of others can be so compellingly internalized that they can hamper making autonomous judgments and actions. The tendency is to think and act like everyone else in their group, for better or worse. Anyone who does not think like them is an outsider, and that is not acceptable to people whose sense of identity and worth comes from the group. That kind of rigidity does not encourage acceptance of others who may hold different views or be in different stages. It is hard for them to welcome the stranger or to accept other points of view.

Following are some questions that can help you ascertain where the tweens are in their development. Affirmative answers to these questions indicate persons may be in the mythic-literal stage:

▶ Do they accept the scriptures as true in a concrete and literal sense, rather than being stories and maxims that may or may not be real or based on evidence or scholarship?
▶ Do they spend a lot of time trying to determine what's real and what's not?
▶ Do they think that they can influence God's actions by being good?

Affirmative answers to these questions indicate persons may be in the synthetic-conventional stage:

▶ Do they have important peer groups or have leaders who are primarily responsible for shaping their faith?
▶ Is it important to them that they understand and follow rules?
▶ Do they insist that everybody play by the rules, including God?
▶ Is their main image of God that of a perfect parent?
(from *Finding Your Religion When the Faith You Grew up With Has Lost Its Meaning*, by Scotty McLennan, Harper San Francisco, 2000.)

Please note and underscore this point: Whatever stage people are in is the best stage for them. Not everyone develops at the same pace and it's possible for people to get stuck in one stage and stay there the rest of their lives. As previously noted, the majority of Americans can best be characterized by the Synthetic-Conventional stage. It is important that teachers and leaders

> ## Whatever stage people are in is the best stage for them.

accept tweens (and all people) where they are and invite them to grow. Understanding the stages of faith help us to provide appropriate learning opportunities for them to succeed. The following sections offer suggestions to guide you as you help others to grow in their faith.

What tweens need for their faith development:

▶ *To develop and practice their thinking skills*
▶ *To be given opportunities to try out different viewpoints in a safe learning environment*
▶ *To develop their sense of belonging to the faith community—the local congregation, a group, and globally*
▶ *To participate in meaningful ways in the community and especially in worship*
▶ *To share what they learn with others at various stages of life*
▶ *To affirm themselves and others as children of God, people of infinite worth*
▶ *To relate faith to the rest of their lives*
▶ *Authentic models who can show them, by example, how to grow in relationship with God, themselves, and others*
▶ *To get to know the Bible better*
▶ *To grow in their understanding of God, others, and themselves*
▶ *Opportunities to practice discipleship*

Erik Erickson said that this stage of life is characterized by the internal struggle between industry and inferiority. Another way to say that is that tweens develop their sense of self worth in large measure by what they do (industry). It is important for them to be good at something.

> Tweens develop their sense of self worth in large measure by what they do.

Success at this stage helps them to believe in themselves and to trust that they have a contribution to make to the world. It also helps them to trust God and to believe that God is with them. They acquire a sense of co-creation with God, which influences their theology. They naturally sense that "I am what I learn," which contributes to their sense of identity. If they don't successfully learn how to make or do something, they may develop feelings of inferiority, which can be self-defeating and have negative implications for future success. In the next section we explore some ways that teachers and leaders can assist tweens in developing their faith.

Ways to structure class sessions:
(and work with students to facilitate their growth)

Dick Murray, who taught at Perkins School of Theology for many years, had a basic approach for teaching the Bible with youth that works equally well for tweens. He said that there are two basic ways to learn. He called them "knowledge about" and "involvement with." Keep that in mind as you think of ways to structure learning opportunities. What do you want them to have knowledge about? What are things that you will involve them in? Here are some things that are appropriate for tweens to learn that will help them grow in their faith.

Tweens should gain knowledge about the history and beliefs of their faith tradition, that is the Church universal, their denomination, and their congregation. In the process of learning history and beliefs, they will learn the meaning of church membership. Stories, videos, games, and songs are good ways for them to develop a sense of belonging, which we've noted is one of the basic human needs. Have guest speakers from your congregation or community come to sessions to tell their faith stories. Tweens' sense of belonging will grow in relationship to the congregation, denomination, and the worldwide church as they experience their relationship with them.

> Have guest speakers from your congregation.

They can learn the names of the books of the Bible and know the different kinds of literature contained in the Bible. It's a good time for them to learn how to use the hymnal, to discover the creeds, prayers, songs, and hymns in it and learn some things about them. Increase their vocabulary of words related to faith. Use study tools such as concordances, maps, and dictionaries to help them learn. Mnemonic strategies such as songs and games can help too.

Provide guidance for prayer and Bible reading. Many leaders provide boxes for students to anonymously place their prayer concerns. Pray together and pray for them. Ask them to pray for you, at your regularly scheduled meetings and in between times. Give them the Bible readings for the coming week from the curriculum resource you use or from the lectionary readings if your church uses them. Covenant with them to read the Bible and pray throughout the week.

> **Provide guidance for prayer and Bible reading.**

Tweens need practice with obedience and their responsibility to the covenantal relationship with God and Church. Read Jeremiah 31:31-34 and Deuteronomy 6: 4-9 with them for biblical examples of how to grow in relationship with God and God's people. Create signs, posters, banners, bookmarks, or other things with these verses on them. Write a class covenant and make copies for each member to keep outlining the shared beliefs and promises to conduct themselves in ways that honor God and keep the Golden Rule. Worship with them as a group; develop your own liturgy or order of worship incorporating these scriptures and their covenant.

More Ways to Work With Tweens

> **Worship with them.**

Worship with them (yes, we've said it before, and we say it again because it is so important). At least once a month, sit together as a group with the larger gathered worshipping congregation. Worship in your classroom, or whatever is your gathering space; see the previous paragraph for specific suggestions. Encourage them to pray and read the Bible at home as well as in the class sessions.

Model the kind of behavior you want tweens to adopt. Benjamin Franklin is reported to have said, "the best sermon is a good example." They may forget the books, the curriculum, and all the details of what you do, but they will never forget you. So be the kind of person you hope that they will be. Be the classic model that will speak to them for a long time. Work on your own spiritual life by practicing spiritual disciplines, participating in Bible studies and mission/outreach projects. Pray with them, pray for them. We aren't saying that you have to be a perfect person to be a good role model. The only perfect person we know is Jesus, and we know that we aren't Jesus Christ, but we can strive to emulate his example by being practicing Christians, "going on to perfection," as John Wesley said.

Tweens need heroes, biblical ones as well as living role models. Besides Jesus and Paul, the Bible is full of people who can be excellent role

Tweens need heroes.

models for tweens. Some possibilities include Esther, Mordecai, David, Jonathan, Jeremiah, Noah, Moses, Abraham, Sarah, Phoebe, Dorcas, Peter, Andrew, John, Luke, Barnabas, Timothy, Ruth, Joshua, Gideon, Deborah, and lots more. Tweens need people they can look up to and they need the Bible to be relevant to their lives. Stories of these biblical heroes can make the Bible come alive in germane and important ways.

Practice spiritual disciplines as ways to develop ongoing, closer relationships with God. Richard J. Foster's classic book, *Celebration of Discipline: The Path to Spiritual Growth*, (Harper San Francisco, 2003) and the accompanying workbook (Foster and James Bryan Smith, Harper San Francisco, 1999), are helpful resources, as is *Soul Tending: Life-Forming Practices for Older Youth and Young Adults* (Kenda Dean, ed., Abingdon, 2002). While these texts are not designed for tweens, the concepts and ideas presented within them can be excellent resources for helping them develop a stronger relationship with God. Look to some of the devotional material from the Upper Room such as Devo Zine or Pockets as well. John Wesley believed that the

Practice spiritual disciplines.

spiritual disciplines could be means of grace by which people come to know God and grow in their relationship with the divine.

Practical Application: Concrete Suggestions for
Activities to Do Immediately

Service learning projects are popular hands-on experiences. There are lots of resources available to help you find or decide on projects to do. One such resource is *Beyond Leaf-Raking: Learning to Serve/Serving to Learn* (Benson and Roehlkepartain, Abingdon, 1993), not that raking leaves wouldn't be a good thing to do. Another is *Tween Time: Fellowship and Service Projects for Preteens* (Wrede, et al, Abingdon, 2003).

One way to decide what to do is to do a gifts and talents survey of your tweens. Develop a pool of ideas based on what they can do and like to do. Don't forget that a service project can be in the church. Combine a couple of tweens' needs by having them be prayer partners with students in a younger class. Have them team-teach a class session with the teacher of a group of younger boys and girls. Go the other direction and have them partner with older adults. Have them illustrate or create a drama to tell a biblical story to another group. As they share their faith with others, they grow more committed to God and have a stronger relationship with God and God's people.

Learn about stewardship by having a clothing drive from their own closets to give to Goodwill, The Salvation Army, a Bethlehem Center, or other organization that works with families in the community. When they get school supplies in the fall, they can get two pads of paper and two sets of pens and donate the second to help kids with fewer resources start the school year well. Several churches have collection baskets that are taken to area schools for administrators to distribute discreetly.

> ## Struggle with moral and ethical dilemmas through role plays.

Struggle with moral and ethical dilemmas through role plays. There are several ready-made resources available that have these, but tweens' own lives are full of ethical dilemmas such as what to do when your best friend cheats on a school test by copying your answers? What do you do when your buddy shoplifts and the store manager asks you if he did it? Role-plays followed by debriefing can help tweens develop their senses of right and wrong in light of Christianity. They can observe and practice the relationship between obedience (listening) and making good choices. In addition, the use of masks, clown make-up and costumes are known ways to help get in touch with real issues while allowing tweens to "save face" behind make-up or a mask.

> **Research shows that mentors, especially one-on-one relationships, are more effective in helping people mature in their faith than any other thing.**

Specifically related to their spiritual formation, research shows that mentors, especially one-on-one relationships, are more effective in helping people mature in their faith than any other thing. You can be a mentor and you can invite others to this special role. Ask the tweens who they think would be good mentors. Invite those people to a session. Plan a retreat to help adults and tweens get a good start on their relationship.

Give your tweens their own journals for drawing and/or writing their reflections. Build in time for them to use them. You may want to create a common journal for your class that different tweens can write in as they feel led.

Give them Bibles that they can read and understand. The King James Version was the common language of 1611; it's nearly 400 years past today's street talk. Even the New King James Version does not speak contemporary language.

We are blessed to have lots of choices today of versions and paraphrases in vernacular language. The Contemporary English Version (CEV), which was recently released by the American Bible Society, was specifically created for people with developing reading levels. Not only is the language easier to understand, but the sentence structures and organization are closer to what tweens experience in school textbooks. It also has pictures, color-coding, charts, and essays to assist their understanding. It's available on CD-ROM, so if you use computers in your program, the CEV is a good choice. So is the New Revised Standard Version. From our conversations with various church leaders, we recommend that young people receive Bibles that don't have cute covers or political slants; rather, give them Bibles that they will use throughout their lives.

> Give them Bibles that they will use throughout their lives.

SUMMARY

Delia Halverson described children's movement through the stages of faith this way:

I need.
I want.
I imagine.
I learn.
I understand.

Many girls and boys start confirmation at this age. While confirmation recognizes persons as adults in the faith community, it is very early in their lives to make such an important decision. Pastors and Christian educators hope that by confirming at this early age, young people will feel connected to the church in a significant, long-lasting way. However, readiness for confirmation should not be measured by a person's grade level in school. Your sensitivity to each one is absolutely necessary. Remember what you have learned about how they develop before you decide when to offer confirmation and who is invited to join. There is a lot to consider.

Tweens think that everything should be fair, including God. Of course, fair is in the eyes of the beholder. They are able to make choices and they are capable of following God's will to the best of their understanding. Teachers and leaders must give them safe times and places to get to know God personally and then to interpret and express the meaning of their relationships with God, others, and themselves. We need to allow them to question and to doubt without judgment, to seek answers, and offer them opportunities to find those answers in real life experiences.

> We need to allow them to question and doubt without judgment.

We must offer them our best and trust them and God to do likewise as they grow in faith throughout their lives.

It is truly a joy to work with tweens and walk alongside them through these steps of their faith journeys. They have so much potential and they have great capacities to love and learn. What could be better than to share your faith with these young seekers who need, want, and grow in their understanding and faith?

> What could be better than to share your faith with these young seekers who need, want, and grow in their understanding and faith?

Chapter Six

TRANSITIONS IN LEARNING STYLES

Introduction

In previous chapters you have learned that most tweens are in what Jean Piaget called concrete operations in their cognitive development. That means that they don't understand metaphors and symbolism very well; what you see is what you get. Be careful what you say because they will take it literally. One adage says, "A young mind is like gelatin. The idea is to put in lots of good stuff before it sets." However, do not think that tween brains are blank slates that you can write on, or banks in which you can simply make deposits. Every time you meet with them, they bring all their life experiences, including all the good and bad learning experiences that they've had thus far in life. They tend to be a little guarded because of the bad experiences, so your honesty and openness to learning with them will go a long way toward building positive relationships with them. Don't think that you can slip anything by them because they seem to have a sixth sense about truth and will call you on anything that sounds phony to them.

> Your honesty and openness to learning with them will go a long way toward building positive relationships with them.

So far this book has helped you understand how tweens develop physically, mentally, emotionally and spiritually. All of this should assist you in making good choices about what and how you teach and how tweens will likely receive it. They need mental challenges that are suitable to their cognitive abilities and opportunities to practice using them.

Since change is the operative word in their development, it should come as no surprise that this is a transitional time in learning for them. Up to this point in their lives, parents, grandparents, and teachers have told them what to think. Now they are asked to think for themselves, to make decisions, and be able to communicate what they think. That's a major transition for them, so it takes some time for them to get the hang of it. It may take you some time to put it all together, too. This chapter intends to help you and them have positive teaching and learning experiences.

Learning Theory: Multiple Intelligences

Dr. Howard Gardner of Harvard University has made one of the most significant contributions to learning theory in recent years. His theory of *multiple intelligences* helps us understand why some people are really good at math, art, music, talking, writing, interpersonal relationships, and intrapersonal relationships. He hypothesized that people have seven or eight different *intelligences*, or ways that they learn. Everyone has at least some of each of these intelligences, but everyone has preferences for how they learn and develops them more fully. These intelligences are called:

▶ *Verbal/linguistic*
▶ *Logical/mathematical*
▶ *Visual/spatial*
▶ *Body/kinesthetic*
▶ *Musical/rhythmic*
▶ *Interpersonal*
▶ *Intrapersonal*
▶ *Religious/natural*

> The brain seems to respond to music.

Gardner says that we most likely develop our musical intelligence first. You may have noticed that a lot of parents play Mozart for their young children, even as early as while children are in the womb! The brain seems to respond to music in ways that increase the brain's ability to develop its logical/mathematical and other intelligences. Here are some things that you can do to experience multiple intelligence theory. The following experience, adapted from one by David Lazear should help you understand how you use your multiple intelligences, which in turn can aid your planning for learning opportunities with your tweens.

TRY THIS: Think of an issue that tweens face. Write it down. Think of a biblical character who faced the same issue. Using a Bible concordance, find the story in the Bible and read it. Then close the Bible. Write the story in your own words, only substitute your name for the name of the biblical character. You can start with that well-known phrase, "Once upon a time," and go on to describe the situation of the character (you/biblical character). Be sure to include all that the character went through before she or he got resolution, and write the ending too. When you are done writing, read it aloud, as if you are experiencing it for the first time. What did you learn about the Bible? What did you learn about yourself? How does writing and reading change your perception of the biblical story and your own experience? The perspective of writing and reading is amazing, often giving new insights into issues. What you've just done is use your verbal/linguistic intelligence to learn something about the Bible and how it can speak to your life.

Make a list of 3-5 issues that you face in your life. One can certainly be the one you wrote about in the previous experience. Group any experiences that have connections or similarities together. Could you build bridges between any of them? Do you need to regroup them? The process of classifying and grouping engages your logical/mathematical intelligence and brings another viewpoint for the issues in your life.

Get a piece of blank paper, some colored pencils or crayons, and that story you wrote in the first experience. Using stick figures or however you can, draw the story. Pretend that you are a cartoonist for a newspaper and draw brief episodes of your story in a series of boxes. Don't worry about being artistic; the main goal here is to express what happened to you in that story. Don't think too much about it or spend too much time on it, go with whatever comes with your first attempt. When you are done, look at your cartoon boxes. Do you get any insights that you did not get in the previous two experiences? You're using your visual/spatial intelligence to add to your understanding of the Bible story and your life.

Now set aside that drawing. Stand up and close your eyes. Make gestures or body movements that express the essence of your story. Make sure that you are in a safe place so that you won't hit anything as you move. Don't worry about looking foolish. If anyone else is in the room, have them close their eyes and do it along with you. Use your body to express any feelings that you associate with the story. Feel the story in your body. If you feel like dancing, by all means, dance! Take your time with this to allow yourself the opportunity to get into it. Don't rush through it. When you are done, sit down, and close your eyes again. In your mind's eye, picture yourself moving through the story with as many details as you can remember. What new awareness do you have from considering the story through your body's movement? Your body/kinesthetic intelligence has helped you experience the story in a new way.

If you were a drummer, what kind of beat would your story have? Come on, haven't you always wanted to play the drums? Beat out that rhythm with your fingers on the surface in front of you. When you've got the beat, imagine what kind of music would go with it. If your story were a song, how would it sound? Do you know any songs that could go with your story? Can you hear a song in your imagination? If you have the music available on CD or tape, find it and play it. If a familiar song doesn't come to mind, maybe original lyrics, rhythms, and melody will play in your head. In any case, listen to the music and beat out the rhythm on the table. You are using your rhythmic/musical intelligence to add another dimension to your learning.

Find someone you trust and tell that person about what you've been experiencing in the previous exercises. Talk about your feelings, your questions, and what you've learned thus far. That person may ask you some questions that will help you to more fully understand your experiences. That's good, because the point is to communicate as fully with the other person as you can. You may have heard people say that they don't realize how they feel about things until they talk them out and hear what they have to say about a subject. That's interpersonal intelligence at work. By talking things out with another person, you get the benefit of knowing what they think and perhaps new understanding of your own.

Here is one more intelligence to experience, but you have to do this one by yourself. Find a quiet, comfortable place where you can close yourself off from the world for a few minutes. Do you remember the film *Back to the Future*? This is sort of a "back to the future" experience that requires your imagination. Get comfortable, take some deep, even breaths, and then close your eyes. Allow your mind to become a movie screen. Think about that biblical story in which you became the hero or main character. Imagine that you are traveling through time into the future maybe a couple hundred years from now. Perhaps you see yourself on Mars or some other planet. You have the perspective of history to look back on your life and the issue in that story you wrote. From the perspective of time, what advice would your future self give to you today? Listen carefully to your future self. Look around that movie screen of your mind for any other clues that could help you deal with that issue you chose for your story and make a mental note to remember them. When you are ready, come back to the current time and space. Take a little time to either jot some notes to yourself or sketch anything you want to remember about what you learned from this imaginary experience. What new insights did you get? Those insights come from your intrapersonal intelligence.

A similar intrapersonal experience is to imagine having a conversation with Jesus about your particular story or issue. Imagine talking to him and listening to him. What does he say? What do you say? Pay attention and ask him to help you. You may choose to write a dialogue of this conversation. By doing so, you use your intrapersonal, interpersonal, kinesthetic, and verbal intelligences to learn about your situation.

Note that everything you've just done is related to a single idea, but you experienced them seven different ways. That is a concrete way to understand multiple intelligence, and everything that you've just done you can do with tweens, because they are in concrete operations cognitively. One way to start is to give each person or team of two a Bible verse or short passage and have them figure out ways to present it using each of the multiple intelligences. Remember that you have more life experience than they do, but they may have more imagination or more logical or artistic abilities than you do.

As the psalmist said, we are "fearfully and wonderfully made" (Psalm 8). We aren't all alike, but all people can learn in many different ways. You can use what you have just experienced and adapt your learning to responding to their needs. They may be a little nervous trying this, but weren't you? Let's start now to apply theory to life.

> We aren't all alike, but all people can learn in many different ways.

TEACHER HELP

What Tweens Need:

Practice with relationships with their peers: Tweens usually do better in groups than working alone; however, keep in mind gender differences as they work together. Boys may feel more comfortable working with boys and girls may feel more comfortable working with girls. Encourage them to bring their friends. Being with them will not only increase your group's size, but also encourages their comfort zones as they interact with you and others.

Success opportunities: Provide an emotionally safe environment for tweens to try things. Remember that they are up and down emotionally with emerging hormones and physical growth spurts, so do not be surprised if one has a meltdown while another enjoys great success with an activity. Provide varieties of activities that offer everyone chances to feel good about themselves and their abilities.

Opportunities to make choices: Offer more than one way to learn a concept and let them choose between two equally valid but different things to do and ways to learn. This is one of the gifts of utilizing multiple intelligence theory. Everyone will have their druthers or preferred ways to do things. They can choose ways to learn that work best for them, or you may challenge them to try several approaches to the same concept. That allows them to stretch mentally and experience things from the perspective of others. They can also choose to be good stewards of all God's gifts.

Mentors: Tweens need positive role models, people who can show them how to work through the challenges they face in their lives right now and those that they will face in the future by the way that they live their lives. You may invite other adults to join you in working with the tweens. Ask the tweens who the people are in the congregation that they look up to and invite them to develop ongoing relationships with these young people. Many churches engage mentors for confirmation, but research shows that partnering younger and older people reaps benefits for people of all ages, including a greater sense of community. Some churches set up ongoing prayer partnerships between older and younger members that are meaningful to young and old alike. Older, middle, and young adults can all be good mentors.

> Ask the tweens who the people are in the congregation that they look up to and invite them to develop ongoing relationships with these young people.

Heroes: In addition to the afore-mentioned mentors, tweens need heroes. Tween time is a great time for girls and boys to learn stories about biblical heroes. The Bible is full of stories of human beings who faced hard decisions and made both good and bad choices. Tweens can learn from their examples. They could do the exercise that you did as described above.

To move: Fred Edie says that asking kids to sit still for an hour is "like asking flies not buzz." (*Sunday School CPR*; Abingdon, 1998). Don't expect them to sit still and talk. They need to move their muscles, and besides that, they learn more if they use more than their ears and mouths.

Hands on, experiential, active learning and reflection time: They need to do things themselves. See the section below to help you plan active, experiential learning lessons. They also need time to think about things. Sometimes in our desire to keep them busy, we don't provide time to "be still and know that I am God" (Psalm 46). Be sure to provide time for them to reflect on their activities, lessons, and their lives.

Opportunities to use their heads, hearts, and hands, to experience and attach themselves to the Holy One, to each other, and to the earth: Like God, we are Trinitarian beings, so we need to use all three aspects of our personhood to fully experience life.

To become better acquainted with the Christian story: Tweens should have their own Bibles, become familiar with the books of the Bible, find Bible references and learn how the Bible came to be. They are ready to understand the concepts of sin, forgiveness, Jesus' death and resurrection, the coming the Holy Spirit, discipleship, Christ's return, heaven, hell, and death. Tweens often have questions about these important aspects of the Christian faith, but do not always get the answers that they need. They need the promises and assurances found in scripture. They have the ability to memorize them. While some adults may think that questions imply disrespect or disbelief, tweens have a natural curiosity and need to know. If they don't find their answers in the church, they will (and do!) look elsewhere, including cults and gangs.

> Sometimes in our desire to keep them busy, we don't provide time to "be still and know that I am God" (Psalm 46).

To be mentors and ministers: Everyone needs to be needed. You might work with a teacher of younger children to set up partnerships between tweens and younger girls and boys and arrange for times that your tweens can assist in Sunday School, Vacation Bible School, or other settings. This allows them to explore and use their abilities and gifts. While mission trips have become popular for youth groups, tweens are not too young to participate in mission work locally or in intergenerational groups.

To worship: Tweens need prayer and they need to learn how to pray the various prayers of praise, thanks, confession, intercession, and petition. This is a good time to teach the various forms of prayer and to give them practice in these forms. They need to be active participating members of the body of Christ.

Bottom line: They need a variety of opportunities and experiences to help them use all their muscles, minds, and spirits to learn.

The Learning Environment

A safe learning environment is a not just an attractive, well-lighted and ventilated space with lots of storage, though these are important. It is also a place with appropriate artwork and curriculum for their ages and stage of life. It welcomes tweens and gives them posted guidelines for appropriate behavior and learning activities. There is a ratio of at least one adult for every eight students. It is a place where girls and boys feel comfortable, where the furniture fits their bodies. A good learning environment is one in which they feel safe trying things out without risking embarrassment or ridicule, and where they experience success and positive self-esteem. Everything teaches, so don't overlook the importance of a colorful, comfortable space that makes them feel good about being there.

> A good learning environment is one in which they feel safe trying things out without risking embarrassment or ridicule, and where they experience success and positive self-esteem.

Along with a safe, inviting space, your preparation and attention to their needs will help make that environment conducive to learning. In the next section, we share some teaching and learning methods that work well with tweens.

Teaching-Learning Methods to Use With Tweens

Experiential Learning

Experiential learning gives tweens hands-on opportunities to try things. It gets their bodies, minds and spirits moving. It also gives them time to think about what they learn from the experience. Here is a short description of experiential learning that you can use whether you have a pre-written curriculum or are creating a new learning experience.

How to learn from an experience:

E—Experience: Do something! Whether spontaneous or planned, experiential learning starts with an interaction of persons with a group or individually provides an opportunity to learn.

I—Identify: Encourage students to look at what they did. Select a specific portion of the experience that you have shared which you would like them to better understand. Isolate and draw the group's attention to it. These questions may help:

▶ What behavior shall we work on?
▶ Let's explore the effect of this (whatever the experience was) on each of us.
▶ What did each of us say? What did we hear? What did we feel as we experienced it?
▶ What non-verbal behavior did we see?

Recall the effects of what happened on them. Their reactions—verbal, non-verbal, and emotional—generate data from these questions that offer further learning.

A—Analyze: Move behind the data just collected from that conversation to deepen their understanding. Invite them to think about what happened as they did whatever the experience was. Determine whether what happened was helpful or a hindrance. Compare the consequences of the whole event with the goals and/or issues that occurred. Do they fit with their typical responses? Interpret their behavior in terms of relationships. These questions may help:

▶ What sense do you make out of this?
▶ How would you interpret this data or experience?
▶ What are the cause and effect relationships within the story or experience? For example: When X happened, A, B, and C resulted.

G—Generalize: Plan for the next time this happens. Draw conclusions by reflecting on the experience and anticipating what to do the next time.

▶ Would you do the same thing again?

▶ What would you do differently? The same?

▶ What can we learn from this?

▶ What are some principles we can use in other experiences?

Repeat these steps for each learning experience. Storytelling is a major way that tweens give unity and value to their experiences, so it is important for them to be able to tell their stories and to talk about their experiences. However, keep in mind that they have short attention spans, so don't belabor any of the steps.

> Storytelling is a major way that tweens give unity and value to their experiences.

Here are a few topics that lend themselves well to experiential learning with tweens. Of course, there are lots more:

▶ Stewardship of the earth, resources, time, energy
▶ Caring, serving others
▶ Devotions, reflection, prayer, worship
▶ Values and morals, ethical decision making
▶ Leadership practice

Cooperative Learning

Cooperative learning is basically working in teams or groups to work on specific tasks or projects. You may think that all education constitutes cooperative learning, but that is not altogether true. We live in a very competitive world that often sets up winners and losers. Tweens especially need to be winners. Cooperative, rather than competitive, learning cuts down on that "loser" mentality that can devastate tweens.

> Cooperative, rather than competitive, learning cuts down on that "loser" mentality that can devastate tweens.

Not only does cooperative learning help with their self-esteem, research shows that tweens actually learn better working together and they get to practice their discussion and interpersonal relationship skills at the same time. They teach each other, which helps them remember the subject as well as the learning experience. Keys to successful cooperative learning include:

▶ Teacher planning
▶ Student engagement
▶ Quality work is essential
▶ Constant student monitoring
▶ Establishing time requirements
▶ Promoting trust, cohesiveness, and responsibility
▶ Assessment to ascertain the outcomes of the learning experience

There are lots of ways to implement cooperative learning, but following are a few suggested methods to incorporate cooperative learning into your setting.

The P-I-E Method

Play is children's work, and as the designation "tweens" indicates, childhood is not as long as it used to be. However, learning can be as easy as "pie" no matter what the age or stage of the learners. The work of learning can be fun.

P = play
I = interactive
E = experiential

As you plan learning activities for tweens, think of fun ways to introduce your topic. Use games. Start a list of games that you can adapt to various learning situations. There are also games that you can buy, and some curricula include games in their lesson plans. Games make learning fun and keep learners guessing.

We don't want our students to have all the fun, so we do whatever they do. We make it a practice never to ask anybody to do anything we wouldn't do ourselves, so we do things with our students. Getting involved with them builds bridges to them. Students see you as a real person, not just an authority figure. Interacting with tweens is fun for them and you, and it shows them that you are a safe, accessible person if they need to talk to an adult who isn't a parent someday. Do not underestimate the importance of that relationship. Research shows that Sunday school teachers and leaders are second only to parents in their influence on how people grow in their faith.

We think that experiential education is more effective than other methodologies. One thing we've learned about how people learn is that the more senses involved in learning, the better they remember what's being taught. John Dewey is credited with saying, "We learn by doing and reflecting on what we do." The combination of doing something that involves our eyes, ears, nose, taste buds, and hands, and taking time to think about the experience is powerful. This chapter includes several ways to show you how to do it. It's true: teaching and learning can be as easy as "pie!"

> Research shows that Sunday school teachers and leaders are second only to parents in their influence on how people grow in their faith.

TPS – Think, Pair, Share:

Here's another cooperative learning method. Have the girls and boys form pairs. Ask a question. Give them a signal to "Think." Allow a few minutes for them to think about their own responses to the question. Signal "Share." An option is to have two pairs of students share their responses with each other, then have the pairs report to the whole group.

The TPS method is good way to develop discussion skills. Hint: pair introverts together and extroverts together. If you pair introverts with extroverts, you may never hear from the introverts. Extroverts will always make sure that they get a chance to talk, and will enter readily into conversation. It's harder for introverts to get started, but eventually the silence will overpower them and one will start talking, thus encouraging the others to participate. Variations on the TPS are Numbered Heads Together and the STAD, which follow.

Numbered Heads Together:

1. Plan your lesson around a problem to solve. Write open-ended questions (questions that cannot be answered in a single syllable) to ask that are related to the problem.

2. Form teams by having the group number off by four or six depending on the size of your group. Have all the 1s, 2s, etc. sit together.

3. Pose questions for each group to answer.

4. Call for "heads together" for them to work together on the questions.

5. Call on numbered respondents to solve the problem. Compare and affirm their responses.

STAD – Student Teams Achievement Divisions

1. Form heterogeneous learning teams.

2. Present the content in whatever way seems appropriate to you. Maybe you will tell a story, present a short play, show a video clip or write questions on a chalk or dry erase board.

3. Have the teams discuss and practice their responses to the content. They might do a role play, write a readers' play or skit, write a song or poem, create a mural, plan a service project, or other response to what you present.

4. Assess the groups' and individuals' mastery as they present what they've learned in response to what you've posed for them.

5. Calculate their improvement and recognize team accomplishments after all groups have presented their responses.

6. Debrief the experience and what they learned.

The MUD Method

Israel Galindo, author of The Craft of Christian Teaching, developed the

MUD method. MUD stands for:

M= memorizing
U= understanding
D= doing

The teacher's role in MUD is to facilitate and encourage students to apply what they learn. You might briefly present the content of a lesson through a short introduction, story, video clip or other presentation. Demonstrations and some object lessons, if not too metaphorical, would also work. You may then divide them into small groups to discuss the content. Keep in mind that this is not tweens' best skill, but that they need opportunities to practice. To assist them, you may supplement their learning experience with worksheets, handouts, or questions to explore. You may ask them to explore the subject, ponder their responses to a question, define, research, compare, contrast, or illustrate it. All of these intend to get them to do things that will increase their understanding of the topic.

LEGO Method

Galindo also created the LEGO method. Use LEGO® toy pieces to represent a problem or mystery that must be solved. Each person gets one LEGO® piece and has to work with others to create some sort of sculpture that represents an answer to a posed problem. Galindo uses LEGO this way:

L=Lecture
E=Experience
G=Groups
O=Outcomes

Here is one example of how to use this method.

L: The teacher or leader gives a brief introduction to define and illustrate the theme for the session. You might present a story, a video clip, a dialogue, or any other way to introduce the theme.

E: Divide the students into pairs and ask them to discuss and respond to what they've heard. Call time and ask for their responses. Put all their responses on the board for everyone to see.

G: The class or group divides into small groups with four persons in each group. Each group works on the next question or builds consensus around responses from pairs, followed by a short debriefing.

O: The teacher shares some content with the whole group, and discusses with them implications and outcomes of their work.

Galindo's approach relies heavily on students' abilities to discuss, but you can modify the approach by making the "E" in the Lego method more experiential. This is a place to use games, role-plays, or other ways for the tweens to get into the content. Outcomes could include having the tweens teach younger girls and boys by developing puppet shows or other things that demonstrate what they have learned.

These are but a few of the teaching methods you can employ for cooperative learning. They will likely inspire you to do more. The benefits of cooperative learning include but are not limited to the following:
► Improved comprehension of basic content
► Reinforcement of social skills
► Student decision making and ownership
► Creation of an active learning environment
► Boosted self esteem
► Celebration of diverse learning styles
► Increased student responsibility
► More success for everyone
► The sheer joy of learning

We hope that you will use cooperative learning with your tweens.

Some Ways to Structure Classes and Learning Environments to Work With Tweens

There's a lot to think about when planning teaching and learning opportunities for tweens. We are fortunate to live in a time when so much research is being done about the brain. We know more about how people learn than we used to know. For example, recent brain research shows that our bodies' need for water may be greater than previously thought.

> ## Some researchers suggest that teachers keep fresh water in classrooms or encourage students to bring water bottles.

Some researchers suggest that teachers keep fresh water in classrooms or encourage students to bring water bottles.

We also know that tweens, as well as others, need changes of pace. Twenty minutes on an activity is about as much as they can handle before they lose interest and zone out. Changing the pace of learning activities helps refocus the brain. Even a short 1-3 minute physical activity such as stretching can change the pace and get them back on task.

As noted earlier, people have several different learning styles and it's important for tweens to have successful experiences. Include a variety of learning styles in your planning to give everyone the chance to succeed. Mix things up. If you have the facilities and time to get them outside, even for a short time, fresh air and the different environment will stimulate learning.

TIC-TAC-TOE

Tweens need structure. Though they will surely test boundaries, they need the assurance of limits that they can count on so that they may explore within a safety zone. One way to provide the structure they need is to be where they need you to be. That's where "Tic-Tac-Toe" can assist you.

> **Tweens need structure.**

Tic-Tac-Toe refers to where you are in relation to them in the learning environment.

> Tic—Teacher in charge,
> Tac—Teacher at the center,
> Toe—Teacher on the edge.

TIC—teacher in charge: That means that the teacher is in front of the group, visible to all, often standing up, presenting a lesson's content. The LEGO method previously mentioned uses the "TIC" structure when the teacher or leader gives a lecture.

TAC—teacher at the center: The teacher is right in the middle of things with the students. Maybe you've decided to do a service-learning project to pack canned goods at a local food bank. You do everything with your tweens, rather than just telling them what to do and standing back while they do it. Another example of "TAC" is worshiping together.

TOE—teacher on the edge: Perhaps you've divided the tweens into small groups. You are available to help them if they need you, but they are engaged in peer or self-directed learning. You are on the edge of the group, not in the front or the middle. .

A combination of all three works well to provide structure and a safe learning environment, as well as changes of pace and style.

"Feeling Into, Meeting With, Responding Out Of"

Dr. Dorothy Jean Furnish, Professor Emeritus of Garrett Evangelical Theological Seminary, created the most easy and accessible way to structure a teaching-learning experience. It works with people of all ages, including tweens. Her three-step approach provides scaffolding upon which you can build any lesson plan. The three steps are "Feeling Into, Meeting With, Responding Out Of."

"Feeling Into" the content or topic for a session helps people make the transition between "getting here" and "being here." Think of warm-up activities to help tweens get settled that also get them ready to meet with the content of your lesson. To use all the teachable moments, plan activities for the first person to arrive. You may have photos to view, quotes on the wall, music playing on a boom box, a game to play, a worksheet to complete; the possibilities are endless. The point is for participants to feel their way into readiness to learn.

> Plan activities for the first person to arrive.

"Meeting With" is what teachers/leaders and participants do when they actually encounter the content for the session. There are many ways to meet with content. You or they may read or tell a Bible story, show a video clip, or read a play or story with people taking various parts. You may have a guest speaker. You may simulate a story or situation. You may pose a problem to be solved. This is a good way to incorporate experiential learning.

"Responding Out Of" begs the question, "So what?" So you and the tweens spent some together engaged in a teaching-learning experience, so what? "Responding Out Of" makes the connection between the content and the rest of their lives. This is the opportunity to make connections and find out what they learned. How will they respond having met with a Bible story? How will they be different? There are as many ways to respond out of a learning opportunity as there are ways to feel into and meet with it. It may be as simple as a question and answer time. It may precipitate a service project. It may result in praying together or individually that God will change and/or

> "Responding Out Of" makes the connection between the content and the rest of their lives.

bless them as they go. "Responding Out Of" helps everyone know that there were good reasons to be together.

This approach allows you to use any method and to structure any teaching-learning situation in a way that works for you. It provides a beginning, middle, and ending to sessions that doesn't leave them or you with the feeling of strings dangling or unfinished business. Here is a way to structure your plans:

Emphasis or Topic:

<u>Feeling Into</u>   <u>Meeting With</u>   <u>Responding Out Of</u>

Practical Application: Things To Do Immediately

Talking:

Tweens need guidance and practice in thinking and communicating. They need an emotionally safe place to practice and participate in Christian community. They need affirmation to build confidence. All of these are related to discussion and interpersonal relationships. Since discussion and developing their relationships with God, others, and themselves are two very important learning goals for tweens, here are some things that you can do right now to assist them.

Tweens need practice and guidelines for how to have discussions. Teachers and other adults often expect them to be able to discuss things, but since they don't know how, they just don't do it. They tend to take turns talking (unless they're talking all at once), but don't listen to each other.

> **They tend to take turns talking (unless they're talking all at once), but don't listen to each other.**

One way to get them started discussing is to use talking sticks or other invitational methods to help them learn how to discuss. The talking stick has its roots in Native American culture. You could use a rock, coin, or other item equally well. Have students sit in a circle. The only person who talks is the one who has the stick in hand. When that person is done talking, he or she passes the stick to another. While it is not a free exchange, it does get everyone into the conversation, and it keeps one or two persons from

> # The talking stick gives everyone the chance to practice both talking and listening.

dominating it. Extroverts will always make themselves heard and introverts will let them. The talking stick gives everyone the chance to practice both talking and listening.

Listening:

Listening is at least as important as talking in discussion, but zoning out is common, as previously mentioned. Teachers and leaders can help tweens develop their discussion skills and relationships by listening to them and helping them learn how to listen to others. Listen to them individually and as a group. Ask them questions about their lives. Let them ask questions about anything that is on their minds no matter how hard it is. And remember that "I don't know" is a legitimate answer to a question. Make your response even better by following up with, "Let's find out together."

Help them develop listening skills by building listening exercises into the time you spend with them. Some suggested activities to practice listening:

Divide the tweens into pairs. Have them interview each other and introduce their partners to the whole group. You may even use microphones and video cameras to set up a news show. They have to listen to each other in order to make the introductions. Not only does this teach listening, but gives them a chance to start building a relationship with a peer.

Strike a triangle or bell and have students listen until they cannot hear it any more. Practice several times with a stopwatch to help them listen more attentively for longer periods of time.

Have them stand in a circle on a hard floor. Drop a pin and see if they can hear it.

Whisper. An old perfume commercial used the phrase, "If you want someone's attention, whisper." Patty experienced its effectiveness as a public school music teacher when she lost her voice every fall after not exercising her vocal chords all summer. When she whispered, so did the students. They had to work harder to hear what was said.

Have a volunteer stand or sit in the center of a circle of participants standing around the volunteer. The volunteer's task is to listen to everything that everyone in circle's perimeter says. Those in the circle are to talk for two minutes about their favorite topics. It really doesn't matter what they say. The important thing is to talk non-stop for two minutes while the person in the center tries to hear everything everyone says. Keep the exercise going for two minutes, which may seem very long for both the talkers and the listener. At the end of the two minutes, ask the listeners to repeat everything that they heard. Let several students be the listener. The experience has several implications, not the least of which is how hard it is to listen in the noisy world in which we live.

Worship:

To grow in relationship with God, themselves and others, tweens need opportunities to worship. Worship should be the centerpiece of Christian life. As tweens worship, they learn to trust God, and practice hospitality as active participants of the gathered faith community. They learn reverence for God and get their basic needs for acceptance and belonging met. They experience the wonder of the Holy One's unconditional love and show their gratitude for all life's blessings. Bible stories engaged in other settings are experienced again as the gathered community re-enacts the Gospel each time it worships together. Worshiping and learning together helps them to trace the story of God's people and the relationship of significant events/individuals to God's activity throughout human history.

> # Worship should be the centerpiece of Christian life.

84

Worship may occur in a variety of settings. Let tweens lead different worship experiences. Ask the pastor and/or worship team leader to invite tweens to help lead parts of worship services, then take time later to debrief the experience with them. Worship in your group setting. Practice parts of the worship service, such as the Lord's Prayer and the Doxology. Encourage them to keep prayer journals.

> ## Let them lead different worship experiences.

Music is not only the first of the multiple intelligences that human beings develop, it is a good way for tweens to worship God. Praise and prayer choruses are easy to learn and sing. Tweens can worship by signing and singing or playing hand bells or other instruments. They might write music or participate through sacred dance.

Working with tweens should involve the parents. We can encourage parents to have family devotions. We may assist them in keeping the Sabbath, teach about family tithing, and invite their family members to join them doing service projects.

Summary

If we are to help tweens in their faith development and spiritual formation, we must listen to them, learn from them, and support them and their parents. We must work on our own spiritual development. We must be attentive to our relationships with God, others, and ourselves. All girls and boys must answer for themselves these questions:

▶ Who is God?
▶ Who am I?
▶ Who are you?
▶ How can I care for all of God's creation?

No one method or curriculum resource has all the answers or solves all the problems you will encounter. Teachers and leaders are part of the curriculum, along with other resources and people. Remember that the more actively involved students are, the greater the possibility of learning. Teaching and learning is a joint venture between students and teachers. Abraham Joshua Heschel once said that we need more text people than textbooks. Years from now, when your current tweens are grown up, they are not likely to remember what curriculum resources you used. They will remember you. From this pivotal, transition time in their lives they will carry memories of the people who helped them grow in their faith.

> Teaching and learning is a joint venture between students and teachers.

Chapter Seven

HELPFUL HINTS AND THINGS TO AVOID

Introduction

Throughout this book we've introduced you to some very special people, the tweens. You have learned about what they are like physically, mentally, emotionally, and spiritually. You have learned some of the issues that these young people face, and that these issues offer you opportunities to help them to learn and grow though them. You have become acquainted with a variety of teaching styles that will assist them to learn. That's a lot! Pat yourself on the back. But if your head is spinning and you're wondering how you're going to remember all of that when you're with them, here's a quick recap and short summary of what we have written in this book.

What Are Tweens Like?

Physically—They have high levels of energy and need to burn it. Girls tend to be further along in their physical development toward womanhood than boys are toward manhood. Tweens are becoming increasingly interested in the opposite sex. They may begin to worry about whether they are "normal."

Emotionally—They are like roller coasters! Up, down, spinning around, sometimes slower than turtles and sometimes it seems that they move at the speed of light. Sometimes they're sweet; sometimes they're sour. What you see is what you get—at that moment. With the physical changes in their bodies come hormonal changes at various times. Some tweens develop very quickly; others are chagrined because they think their bodies are too childlike. Many tweens struggle with their sense of identity. They may begin to experiment with sex, alcohol, and other drugs, especially if their friends are doing it.

> What you see is what you get—at that moment.

Cognitively—Tweens are still concrete in the way that they think about the world. They do not understand metaphors and analogies very well until they get closer to the teen years. They have the ability to classify and organize things, and they have a voracious capacity to learn, especially by making things. They will test rules and limits. They are beginning to develop ideals and identify with role models.

Spiritually—Tweens have great potential to grow spiritually. Most are in the mythic-literal stage, meaning that they mostly understand God in concrete, human terms. Some are transitioning to the synthetic-conventional stage when their experience of God is much like everybody else's that they know. Their concept of God is that God knows and controls all, so they have a great deal of awe for the mystery of God.

Do:

▶ Use active learning methods that let tweens burn their energy in positive ways.

▶ Honor the various ways that people learn by using a variety of teaching and learning methods and multiple intelligences so that everyone has the chance to succeed.

▶ Take time to get to know them and their parents. Listen hard. Listen a lot! They need to be heard and learn how to listen. Encourage families to do things together, especially worship together and really listen to each other.

> **Take time to get to know them.**

▶ Visit the schools that they attend. Have lunch with them and their friends if the schools allow it.

▶ Go to their school activities and other things in which they are involved. Tweens are very busy people, involved in school and civic activities, sports and music. Let them know that you care by showing up at something outside of church. It means a lot to them, even if they never tell you.

▶ Let them make good decisions by providing helpful parameters that set them up for success.

▶ Provide opportunities to practice leadership and interpersonal relationship skills. They learn by doing. You are educating the leaders of the world. Let them take responsibility for leadership with each other and with people of other ages. They aren't just the church of tomorrow; they are the church today.

▶ Provide concrete opportunities for them to practice their faith and use what they know to serve God and others. Get them involved in ministry and mission now.

▶ Remember that though they have remarkable vocabularies, may have "street smarts," and experience many things vicariously through television and computers, they may not be as mature and sophisticated as they appear or sound. Allow them the flexibility to try things. Allow them the time to be kids.

> ## Allow them the time to be kids.

▶ Make sure they have appropriate adult supervision, especially with media and the internet.

▶ Help parents connect with other parents and if possible, provide a time for parents to talk with each other and to practice listening and parenting skills.

▶ Encourage other adults, like yourself and parents, to be involved in all aspects of the tween life, including peer relationship building.

▶ Be sensitive to the transitions around school changes, and their need for things to count on in the midst of change.

Don't:

▶ put shy or introverted students on the spot to read or talk in front of the group.

▶ put an introvert in a group with all extroverts. They won't speak and everyone will miss the contributions that they have to make.

▶ expect kids to suddenly know how to have a discussion just because they know how to talk. Provide opportunities for them to practice their verbal and relational skills in non-threatening ways.

▶ expect consistency from them, but do provide it for them. Since they are changing so fast, they need to be able to depend on the significant people in their lives.

▶ encourage one on one dating or opposite sex pairing, but do focus on group activities.

▶ expect overnight results. Life and learning are processes that reflect the old Shaker dance: two steps forward, one step back. Sometimes tweens will surprise you by how mature they are, and other times exhibit immature behavior. That's normal.

▶ provide junk food. Tweens have enough health issues without the church providing more junk food. Instead, provide tasty, nutritious snacks and plenty of water. They are always hungry and their brains need water.

▶ encourage competitive team games; that time will come quickly enough (see "The American Athlete, Age 10." *Sports Illustrated*, 10/6/03)

Research gathered by the Carnegie Council on Adolescent Development and published in their publication, *Turning Points: Preparing American Youth for the 21st Century*, outlines the key elements of a developmentally responsive educational program for tweens. Included in their recommendation are these elements:

▶ a community for learning
▶ an identified core of common knowledge
▶ ensuring success for all students
▶ empowerment of teachers
▶ preparation of tweens by teachers for the middle grades
▶ better health and fitness

▶ engaging families in the education of young adolescents

▶ connecting schools (church) with communities.

These are all things that the church can develop so that the experience of tweens will be positive and rewarding.

Summary

An adage from education says, "I don't care how much you know until I know how much you care." It's obvious that you care a lot because you read this book and you're working with tweens. It may be a while until they realize what a great gift you've given by being their teachers or leaders, so allow us. On behalf of the tweens, their families, and the church, thanks for being there for them. Thanks for caring about them. Thanks for being faithful to Jesus' command to make disciples of all. Thanks for being a partner in ministry with the tweens, with their parents, their communities, and with us.

The preteen age of the tweens is one of great potential. They aren't little kids any more. They are on their way toward becoming teenagers and adults. It's a great time of life and it is a joy to be with them. We know that God will bless you and them in tween time and beyond.

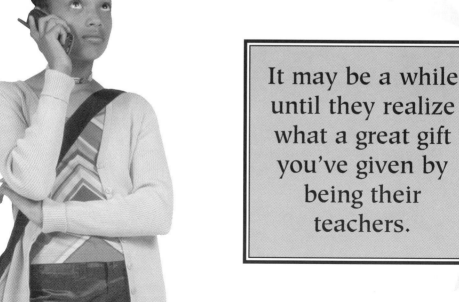

> It may be a while until they realize what a great gift you've given by being their teachers.

REFERENCES

Benson, Peter and Eugene Roehlkepartain. *Beyond Leaf Raking: Learning to Serve/Serving to Learn*. Nashville: Abingdon Press. 1993.

Dean, Kenda (ed.). *Soul Tending: Life-Forming Practices for Older Youth and Young Adults*. Nashville: Abingdon Press. 2002.

Edie, Fred. *Sunday School CPR*. Nashville: Abingdon Press. 1998.

Elkind, David. *The Hurried Child: Growing up too Fast too Soon.* New York: Da Capo Press. 2001.

Elkind, David. *Child Development and Education: A Piagetian Perspective.* Oxford University Press. 1976.

Erickson, Erik and Jean M. Erickson. *The Life Cycle Completed.* New York: W. W. Norton. 1998

Foster, Richard J. *Celebration of Discipline* (25th anniversary edition). Harper San Francisco. 2003

Foster, Richard J. and James Bryan Smith. *A Spiritual Formation Workbook—Revised Edition: Small Group Resources for Nurturing Christian Growth.* Harper San Francisco. 1999.

Fowler, James. *Stages of Faith: The Psychology of Human Development.* Harper San Francisco. 1995

Galindo, Israel. *The Craft of Christian Teaching*. Valley Forge, PA: Judson Press. 1998.

Gilbert, Anne. *Age Group Characteristics*. Brae, CA: Educational Ministries, Inc. 1991.

Gottman, John M. and Jeffrey G. Parker (eds.). *Conversations of Friends: Speculations on Affective Development.* Cambridge University Press. 1987.

Halverson, Delia. *Helping Your Child Discover Faith*. Valley Forge, PA: Judson Press. 1982.

Harris, Maria. *Fashion Me a People*. Louisville: Westminster John Knox Press. 1989.

Kreider, Eugene C. *I Want to Be a Teacher: A Ten-Session Course for New Church School Teachers*. Minneapolis: Augsburg Publishing House. 1981.

Lazear, David and Howard Gardner. *Eight Ways of Knowing, 3rd Edition*. Glenview, IL: Pearson Skylight Professional Development. 1998.

McLennan, Scotty. *Finding Your Religion When the Faith You Grew up With Has Lost Its Meaning*. Harper San Francisco. 2000.

Melton, Joy T. *Safe Sanctuaries: Reducing the Risk of Child Abuse in the Church*. Nashville: Discipleship Resources. 2003.

Mintle, Linda S. Ph.D. "Help Your Tweener Be a Cosmic Girl, Not a Cosmo Girl." http://www.crosswalk.com/family/634198.html.

Osmer, Richard R. *Teaching for Faith*. Louisville: Westminster John Knox Press. 1992.

Piaget, Jean and Barbara Inhelder. *The Psychology of the Child*. New York: Basic Books. 1969

Roche, A. F. "Secular Trends in Human Growth Maturation and Development." *Monographs of the Society for Research in Child Development* #179.

Santrock, John W. *Children* (editions four through seven). New York: McGraw-Hill.

---. *Child Development* (editions seven through ten). New York: McGraw-Hill.

---. *Adolescence* (editions six through nine). New York: McGraw-Hill.

As I was writing my (Ed's) portions of this text I realized how dependent on and thoroughly familiar I am with John Santrock's introductory texts on children and adolescents. I have used his texts as text books every year for over ten years. Much of my own thinking has been shaped by Santrock's categories and his way of outlining material. All of the above texts sit on my shelves and are well-worn. Although none were consulted directly during the writing of this text, I am forever indebted to his work.

Schultze, Quentin J. *Winning Your Kids Back From the Media*. Downers Grove, IL: Intervarsity Press. 1994.

Anchor, Roy M., et al. *Dancing in the Dark: Youth, Popular Culture, and the Electronic Media*. Grand Rapids: Eerdmans Publishing. 1991

Selman, Robert L. *The Growth of Interpersonal Understanding: Developmental and Clinical Analyses*. Philadelphia: Academic Press. 1980.

Stoner, Marcia J. *Tween Spirituality: Offering Opportunities in Preteen Spiritual Growth*. Nashville: Abingdon Press. 2003.

Wilcox, Mary. Poster: "Faith in Search of Understanding." Denver: Living the Good News. 1986.

Wrede, James., Leigh L. Gregg, Mark Bushor, and James Ritchie. *Tween Time: Fellowship and Service Projects for Preteens.* Nashville: Abingdon Press. 2003

Yecke, Cheri Pierson. *The War Against Excellence*. Westport, CT: Praeger. 2003.